About Island Press

Since 1984, the nonprofit Island Press has been stimulating, shaping, and communicating the ideas that are essential for solving environmental problems worldwide. With more than 800 titles in print and some 40 new releases each year, we are the nation's leading publisher on environmental issues. We identify innovative thinkers and emerging trends in the environmental field. We work with world-renowned experts and authors to develop cross-disciplinary solutions to environmental challenges.

Island Press designs and implements coordinated book publication campaigns in order to communicate our critical messages in print, in person, and online using the latest technologies, programs, and the media. Our goal: to reach targeted audiences—scientists, policymakers, environmental advocates, the media, and concerned citizens—who can and will take action to protect the plants and animals that enrich our world, the ecosystems we need to survive, the water we drink, and the air we breathe.

Island Press gratefully acknowledges the support of its work by the Agua Fund, Inc., The Margaret A. Cargill Foundation, Betsy and Jesse Fink Foundation, The William and Flora Hewlett Foundation, The Kresge Foundation, The Forrest and Frances Lattner Foundation, The Andrew W. Mellon Foundation, The Curtis and Edith Munson Foundation, The Overbrook Foundation, The David and Lucile Packard Foundation, The Summit Foundation, Trust for Architectural Easements, The Winslow Foundation, and other generous donors.

The opinions expressed in this book are those of the author(s) and do not necessarily reflect the views of our donors.

THE SHAPE OF GREEN

THE SHAPE OF GREEN

Aesthetics, Ecology, and Design

LANCE HOSEY

⬤ ISLANDPRESS Washington | Covelo | London

Library of Congress Cataloging-in-Publication Data

Hosey, Lance.
  The shape of green : aesthetics, ecology, and design / Lance Hosey.
    p. cm.
  Includes bibliographical references.
  ISBN 978-1-61091-031-6 (cloth : alk. paper) — ISBN 1-61091-031-1 (cloth : alk. paper)
— ISBN 978-1-61091-032-3 (pbk. : alk. paper) — ISBN 1-61091-032-X (pbk. : alk. paper)
1. Sustainable design. 2. Sustainable architecture. 3. Green technology. 4. Aesthetics. 5.
Sustainability. 6. Environmentalism. I. Title.
  NK1520 .H672012
  745.2—dc23   2011049246

Printed using Minion

Text design by Maureen Gately
Typesetting by Sztrecska Publishing

 Printed on recycled, acid-free paper

Manufactured in the United States of America
10 9 8 7 6 5 4 3 2 1

Keywords: architectural design, biomimicry, biophilia, corporate style, circumstantial
style, e-waste, ecological design, energy-efficient design, environmental design, epochal
style, fractal, green architecture, happy product index, history-based form, industrial
design, market-based form, nature, place-based form, populist style, regional style,
self-sustaining form, sustainability, thermal comfort, urban design, urban ecology

Note: The background image on page 34 shows a Shinkansen 500 Bullet Train.
The background image on page 125 shows a serpentine garden wall at the
University of Virginia that was designed by Thomas Jefferson.

For my brothers,
who were there
when I woke up

It is only shallow people
who do not judge by appearances.
The true mystery of the world is the visible,
not the invisible.
—*Oscar Wilde*

Table of Contents

1 | The Sustainability of Beauty

*Nature has never been silent for me. Nature whispers in my
ear all the time, and it is the same thing over and over. It is
not "Love." It is not "Worship." It is not "Psst! Dig here!"
     Nature whispers, and sometimes, shouts, "Beauty,
beauty, beauty, beauty."*

—*Sharman Apt Russell*

DESIGN IS SHAPE WITH PURPOSE.

In recent years, industry has begun to reconsider its purposes. Can products be better for people? Can buildings be better for the planet? Can companies be environmentally responsible and still turn a profit? Addressing these questions is causing dramatic changes in every area of work and life. Yet, as

1

we seek answers to questions about purpose, questions about shape remain. Of the traditional criteria for judging design—cost, performance, and aesthetics—the agenda known as *sustainable design* is redefining the first two by expanding old standards of value. But what about aesthetics? Does sustainability change the face of design or only its content?

Many designers show little interest in this question, and some dismiss it altogether. "[The term] 'green' and sustainability have nothing to do with architecture," architect Peter Eisenman said in a 2009 interview. Designers care about image, and the green movement, like it or not, has a reputation for being all substance and no style. In 2010, design critic Alice Rawsthorn sized up the Leaf, Nissan's celebrated electric car: "It is as dull in style as most gas-guzzling clunkers." Many believe sustainability deals exclusively with energy efficiency, carbon emissions, and material chemistry—issues that belong in a technical manual, not on a napkin sketch. Nuts and bolts are not exactly the stuff of every designer's dreams. As a result, many consider *great design* and *green design* to be separate pursuits, and in fact much of what is touted as "green" is not easy on the eyes. The ugly truth about sustainable design is that much of it is ugly.

Even the most ambitious sustainable design can be unattractive because attractiveness isn't considered essential to sustainability.

Conventional wisdom portrays green as not just occasionally but inevitably unattractive, as if beauty and sustainability were incompatible. "Sustainability and aesthetics in one building?" asked the *San Francisco Chronicle* in 2007. "Is 'well-designed green architecture' an oxymoron?" mused the *American Prospect* in 2009. The previous year, famed journalist Germaine Greer declared, "The first person to design a gracious zero carbon home will have to be a genius at least as innovative and epoch-making as Brunelleschi," referring to the Italian Renaissance architect who engineered the magnificent dome of Florence's Duomo. Green lacks grace, say the critics.

The eco-design movement began with an implied mantra: *If it's not sustainable, it's not beautiful.* Waste spoils taste. Even now, the battle cry continues. "Look at the architecture of the last 15 years," architect James Wines complained in 2009. "It's been more flamboyant and more wasteful than it's ever been before. To build any of these buildings by Frank Gehry [the architect famous for sculptural structures of crumpled metal], it takes . . . 60 to

80 percent more metal and steel and construction than it would to enclose that space in a normal way . . . Mind-boggling waste." Wines suggests that the work of Gehry, the most renowned architect of our time, isn't great design because it's negligent.

Yet the opposing view insists that focusing exclusively on environmental stewardship is just as irresponsible. "Some of the worst buildings I have seen are done by sustainable architects," Eisenman said in the aforementioned interview. "'Sustainable architecture,'" wrote critic Aaron Betsky in 2010, "justifies itself by claiming to be pursuing a higher truth—in this case that of saving the planet. The goal justifies many design crimes, from the relatively minor ones of the production of phenomenally ugly buildings . . . to the creation of spaces and forms that are not particularly good for either the inhabitants or their surroundings."

In the apparent tug-of-war between sustainability and beauty, which should win? *Contract* magazine's 2008 interiors awards jury remarked that the Haworth furniture showroom in Washington, DC, "shows you can create something that's environmentally sensitive but doesn't look like it." In other words, looking green looks bad, so hide it, dress it up. The online design magazine *Inhabitat* proclaims that designer Yves Béhar's projects "have always exhibited a deft balance between stunning aesthetics and sustainable design." Beauty and sustainability need to be *balanced,* as if designing green requires a compromise or trade-off with looking good. Another Web site refers to "the constant battle between aesthetics and sustainability," as if the two unavoidably conflict. "A sophisticated building in an environmental sense is not ipso facto a sophisticated building in a design sense," says architect Eric Owen Moss. "I wouldn't mix the two." Environmental sophistication and design sophistication don't blend well.

Recent surveys confirm how widespread this impression is. In 2010, *Vanity Fair* asked ninety leading architects to pick the "greatest buildings of the past 30 years." Fifty-two people responded, and among the twelve picks with more than a few votes each was a glaring lack of exemplary green projects. (The winner, with nearly three times the number of votes of the second-place choice, was Gehry's Guggenheim Museum in Bilbao, Spain—the epitome of what Wines calls "mind-boggling waste.") Sustainability, it seems, is not much on the minds of the architectural elite.

To test this theory, I conducted my own poll. For my column in *Architect* magazine, I asked 150 experts to pick the most important examples of sustainable design from the same period; to be consistent, we published the

"Green" Design or "Good" Design?
Renzo Piano Building Workshop,
California Academy of Sciences,
San Francisco, California.
Green experts named this the most
important building since 2000.
The architectural elite did not.

first fifty-two replies. The differences were dramatic. Not one building from the *Vanity Fair* list recurred in the top twenty results of my survey, and not a single American architect appeared in both sets of winners. (Of the two architects who did—Italian Renzo Piano and Briton Norman Foster—*Vanity Fair* featured their older, less environmentally ambitious work.) In fact, none of the winners of the first poll appear anywhere on the entire list of 122 projects in the second. Clearly, standards of design excellence and of environmental performance don't match, for the "greatest" buildings of our time are far from the "greenest," and vice versa.

No surprise there. Originally, the concept of sustainability promised to broaden the purpose of contemporary design, specifically by adding ethics to aesthetics, but instead it has virtually *replaced* aesthetics with ethics by providing clear and compelling standards for one and not the other. The most widely accepted measures for environmental performance exclude basic

> Can we be as smart about how things *look* as we are about how they *work?*

considerations about image, shape, and form. Even the most ambitious sustainable design can be unattractive because attractiveness isn't considered essential to sustainability.

But this will change. "It may be true that one has to choose between ethics and aesthetics," wrote the film director Jean-Luc Godard, "but whichever one chooses, one will always find the other at the end of the road." As the green agenda becomes more popular, more designers are realizing that, as Béhar has put it, "virtuous products don't have to equate with indifferent design." Over the past handful of years, plenty of striking examples of eco-design have appeared, and suddenly sustainability is sexy. Yet, what makes these designs look good usually has nothing to do with what makes them green. "Sustainability has, or should have, no relationship to style," insists architect Rafael Viñoly. Fundamental decisions about appearance often are decided by the personal taste of the designers, so when it comes to aesthetics, sustainable design is business as usual.

What if we created a different approach to aesthetics, one based on intelligence and not intuition? Can we be as smart about how things *look* as we are about how they *work?* Typical sustainable design strategies stem from painstaking research and time-tested evidence, and this approach can guide both technical choices and aesthetic choices. For every study demonstrating the benefits hidden inside particular materials and production methods, there are other studies showing how certain shapes, patterns, images, colors, or textures can create environmental, social, and economic value. Why aren't they more familiar to designers?

Although green techniques often seem complicated, actually they could be divided into two simple categories: those you see and those you don't. *INVISIBLE green*—considerations such as embodied energy, material sources, chemical content, and so forth—has become a more familiar agenda, partly because these factors are easier to regulate and measure (and possibly because they don't threaten artistic freedom). Many designers restrict environmental performance to these factors alone; in the words of architect Cesar Pelli, "Sustainability doesn't necessarily photograph." But *VISIBLE green*—form, shape, and image—can have an even greater impact on both conservation and comfort. How a building is shaped can have an enormous effect on how it performs, and some sources estimate that up to 90 percent of a product's environmental impact is determined during the early design phases, prior to decisions about technical details. In other words, elementary decisions about shape—the "look and feel" of a design—are essential to sustainability.

Love It or Lose It

Aesthetics, or sensory appeal, are not just icing on the cake. In both nature and culture, shape and appearance can directly affect success and survival. From a single cell to the entire planet, much of nature can be explained in terms of geometry alone. The filled donut of a blood cell is perfectly streamlined for fluid dynamics. The slight angle of the earth on its axis creates the four seasons, which have helped shape nearly every living creature. And many of these creatures thrive on being attractive—feathers are colorful, flowers are scented, fruit tastes sweet. Life is alluring, and pleasure drives evolution.

The same applies to design—form affects performance, image influences endurance. A square wheel won't work, regardless of how well it's engineered. And even with the most sophisticated mechanical system, a building facing west is going to get hot. So shape affects efficiency but also longevity, which can depend almost completely on visual and emotional appeal. How long will something last if it fails to excite the spirit and stir the imagination? Picture two objects. One uses energy conservatively but is dull, unsightly, or uncomfortable. The other is gorgeous but a glutton for fossil fuels. Which is more likely to endure—the responsible one or the ravishing one?

In *The Botany of Desire,* Michael Pollan shows that domesticated plants and animals have thrived because they have an important survival advantage over their competitors in the wild: *we like them.* Pollan writes: "Human desires form a part of natural history in the same way the hummingbird's love of red does, or the ant's taste for the aphid's honeydew. I think of them as the human equivalent of nectar." The fate of many things depends on whether they please people. Wolves might seem heartier than dogs, but there are 50 million dogs in the world and only ten thousand wolves. Which has adapted better? This view of nature may give you pause—should other species exist just to please us? But as a principle for design, it is essential. If you want something to last, make it as lovable as a Labrador.

Because, as studies show, we form positive associations with things we consider beautiful, we are more likely to become emotionally attached, giving them pet names, for instance. We personalize things we care about. Experiments in interaction design also reveal that people generally consider attractive products more functional than they do unsightly ones and therefore are more apt to use them. We prefer using things that look better, even if they aren't inherently easier to use. Consider the ramifications—if an object is more likely to be used, it's more likely to continue being used. Who throws out a thing they find functional, beautiful, and valuable all at once? A more attractive design discourages us from abandoning it: if we want it, we won't waste it.

> "In the end, we conserve only what we love."
>
> —*Baba Dioum*

Long-term value is impossible without sensory appeal, because if design doesn't inspire, it's destined to be discarded. "In the end," writes Senegalese poet Baba Dioum, "we conserve only what we love." We don't love something because it's nontoxic and biodegradable—we love it because it moves the head and the heart. If people don't want something, it will not last, no matter how thrifty it is. And when our designs end up as litter or landfill, how prudent have we been? "The more clearly we can focus our attention on the wonders and realities of the universe about us," wrote Rachel Carson half a century ago, "the less taste we shall have for destruction." When we treasure something, we're less prone to kill it, so desire fuels preservation. Love it or lose it. In this sense, the old mantra could be replaced by a new one: *If it's not beautiful, it's not sustainable.* Aesthetic attraction is not a superficial concern—it's an environmental imperative. Beauty could save the planet.

Magical Union

In its simplest definition, the word *beauty* refers to sensory pleasure. Our first response to the environment happens not through our minds but through our bodies. Understanding usually comes from perception, often from vision alone, for what you see really is what you "get." Because we interact with the world through its sights, sounds, scents, tastes, and textures, emotion can outweigh intellect. As Carson put it in *The Sense of Wonder,* when encountering nature "it is not half so important to know as to feel." In an eastern Sierra aspen grove in late September, summer bleeds into fall, and I'm surrounded by shimmering leaves of reddish gold, as if I'm walking through a sunset. My first thoughts are not about the chlorophyll draining from the leaves and their ebbing ability to produce oxygen, absorb carbon, and photosynthesize. No, my first reaction is simpler—the sheer splendor of the scene stops me in my tracks. I'm awestruck.

This is why the American conservation movement has worked to preserve natural beauty as our national heritage. In the Sierras, wrote photographer and activist Ansel Adams, we "enter the wilderness and seek, in the primal patterns of nature, a magical union with beauty." Design attuned to nature creates this magical union, celebrating the natural and cultural environments as one world. Now that the ethical value of green design is becoming more accepted and understood, its aesthetic value demands greater attention, for only by embracing both will it live up to its true potential. Sustainable design must offer more to meet the eye—and the ear, the nose, and the skin. If design is to act like nature, it should take our breath away.

In his famous line from *My First Summer in the Sierra*, naturalist John Muir summed up the fundamental principle of ecology: "When we try to pick out anything by itself, we find it hitched to everything else in the Universe." The lesson of ecology applies to culture as much as to nature, for everything we make, regardless of material or medium, is hitched to everything else. Ecology obliges us to think of design as a continuous stream of influence at every scale. Architect Eliel Saarinen advised designers to consider every object within its next larger context—a chair within a room, a room within a house, a house within a street, and so on. This applies in both directions, larger and smaller, like Russian nesting dolls but with a looser fit. The difference between products and interiors is the difference between a desk and

> Aesthetic attraction is not a superficial concern—it's an environmental imperative. Beauty could save the planet.

a "workstation." The difference between architecture and urban planning is the difference between a facade and a street wall. A building doesn't stop at its face, a site doesn't cease at the property line, and a town doesn't end at the city limits.

Reading this book, you might be relaxing in your favorite chair. How comfortable you are—and how much energy is used to make you comfortable—can depend on the size, shape, and color of the text on the page; the texture, proportions, and weight of the book against your hands; and the form and fabric of the chair fitting your body. Your comfort might also rely on the light and breeze coming through the window, which depend on the location of the room within the house and the orientation of the house itself. And these rely on the location of the house on the street, the alignment of the street in the neighborhood, the placement of the neighborhood in its community, and the relationship of the community to the area's climate, altitude, topography, and vegetation, all of which connect to where you're sitting on the earth at large. Just curling up with a book, you encounter the results of many decisions that have shaped the world around you.

At every scale of experience, shape is critical to environmental performance and human response. Yet, as this chapter has shown, aesthetics generally are not considered relevant to sustainable design, and, in fact, sustainability often is considered antithetical to beauty. With this book, I hope to create—for the first time, I believe—a philosophy and methodology for the aesthetic dimensions of sustainable design. Here's the basic argument:

- Not only are aesthetics and sustainable design not opposed to each other, they should, in fact, be considered intricately bound together, for beauty is inherent to the definition and principles of sustainability (chapter 2).
- What's needed is not a superficial or individual approach to style but, instead, a clear set of principles for the aesthetics of ecology (chapter 3).
- Conventional sustainable design strategies have evolved out of in-depth research and tried-and-true evidence about what works and what doesn't, and a similar scientific method can be applied to aesthetics. Designers can create a more rational approach to beauty by combining recent advances in material techniques with decades of research in environmental psychology and millennia of wisdom about the graceful interaction of people and place (chapters 3 to 5).
- This knowledge can inform the development of design at every scale, from products to buildings to cities (chapters 6 to 8).

- These ideas have consequences for designers' habits, values, and standards, but they also connect to humanity's fundamental relationship with the earth, so this topic has significant implications beyond the design industry (chapter 9).
- Sustainability isn't all rocket science, and all designers can promote its basic principles in everything they make (epilogue).

In these chapters, not every example I offer is "green" in a conventional sense. Instead, the pages ahead offer a variety of ideas and designs that together suggest a broader, more inclusive approach to sustainability that I hope will expand the dialogue about how design can promote a better world.

Following the principles of ecology to their logical conclusion could result in revolutions of form as well as content in every industry at every scale, from the hand to the land. Reversing the devastation of nature requires reversing the devastation of culture, for the problem of the planet is first and foremost a human problem. We created the crisis, but we can correct it—by appealing to both morality and sensuality, to both sense and spirit, together. Designers can promote sustainability by embracing what they have always cared about most: the basic shape of things.

**Beauty's Triple Bottom Line.
Evidence shows the following:**

Social. The High Line, New York.
*Richly landscaped places can encourage
socialization, lower crime rates, and promote
well-being, and iconic design can
enhance community identity.*

Economic. Seattle Public Library.
*A single compelling structure can increase
property values and even improve an
entire region's economy.*

Environmental. Bryant Park, New York.
*Well-designed places are better cared for
and discourage abuse, and attractive
receptacles can lower litter rates.*

2 | **The Aesthetic Imperative**

Everybody needs beauty as well as bread.

—*John Muir*

IN NOVEMBER 2009, the cover story of *Scientific American* beckoned to me from a newsstand: "A Plan for a Sustainable Future." Yes! Finally, all the answers concisely laid out in one thin volume. Upon closer inspection, alas, I found the subtitle in smaller print: "How to get all energy from wind, water, and solar power by 2030." Does a "sustainable future" mean merely ridding the world of greenhouse gases?

Instinctively, we feel that sustainability must encompass more than that. In this chapter, I show that embedded in the very concepts of ecology and sustainability is an aesthetic mandate—an imperative toward beauty, pleasure, joy. Yet, popular views of the environmental crisis define both the questions and the answers narrowly—the problem is global warming, the cause is emissions from outmoded energy mechanisms, and the solution is smarter mechanisms. Technology has hijacked sustainability. The clearest statement of this view came from George W. Bush in his 2006 State of the Union address: "America is addicted to oil. The best way to break this addiction is through technology." Yet, our addiction isn't to oil but to consumption, so this view confuses food with appetite. And, to shift the metaphor, believing new tools will break this addiction is like trying to kick a heroin habit with better needles.

"Is it progress if a cannibal uses a fork?" quipped the poet Stanisław Jerzy Lec. Do smarter tools merely make us better at making things worse? As governor of California, Arnold Schwarzenegger commissioned a custom-made, hydrogen-powered Hummer and immediately became the poster boy for alternative fuel. Its emissions weren't carbon but steam—*hasta la vista,* CO_2. Yet, a Hummer measures ten by sixteen feet, so it can't easily squeeze into standard road lanes or parking spaces, and technically it's illegal on many streets. (General Motors discontinued the line in 2010.) Thoroughly accommodating the Hummer would mean fattening up every freeway, parking lot, and garage—a complete overhaul of infrastructure with a huge influx of concrete and asphalt. If everyone drove one—even a gas-free one—the world would burst at the seams. Arnie's engine might be a green dream, but the rest of the Hummer is an environmental nightmare.

Design trumps technology.

Although the hydrogen Hummer was a one-of-a-kind showpiece, consumer eco-cars also tend to rely on their inner workings, not their outer appearance. The 2010 Honda Civic Hybrid—versions of which took two of the top three slots in the American Council for an Energy-Efficient Economy (ACEEE) ranking of the "greenest cars" on the market—is indistinguishable from the conventional Honda Civic. What makes it green is hidden under the hood.

When the Toyota Prius—"the best-loved and most efficient hybrid in America," according to advertisements—entered the American market in 2001, it looked a lot like Toyota's other brands and any number of box sedans on the road that year. Take away the motor, and it's just another car. In fact, compared to the Toyota Corolla, declared the Auto Channel, the Prius styling was "most remarkable for being unremarkable." Yet, the same review hailed

it as the birth of the twenty-first-century car. "If the Toyota Prius points to the automotive future, the future looks good." How could they tell, when the future apparently looked just like the past?

But the 2004 Prius is the iconic model. It grew by six inches and 150 pounds, but its new Kamm-tail teardrop body cut wind resistance enough to improve the fuel economy by 5 miles per gallon, and its drag coefficient (0.25) is among the lowest of any mass-produced car. Design—specifically the shape of the chassis—made up for the additional size and weight. With the Prius revamp, the future of design did begin to look a little brighter.

Nevertheless, its unconventional appearance led critics to call the Prius "a brick on wheels" and "a clumsy looking toad of a car." Regardless of opinion, the real distinction of the redesign was that it didn't look like other cars, and its newly identifiable shape allowed it to become a green status symbol. Now the image of the Prius relates as much to marketability as it does to aerodynamics. As one auto critic wrote of the 2010 model, "Toyota has created the most instantly recognizable hybrid car on the market today and it wasn't going to lose that image" with a redesign. Within a handful of years, the 2004 innovations in shape had become a branding gimmick.

I drive a first-generation Smart Car, which is significantly more fuel efficient than the larger, heavier American model, introduced in 2008. With a conventional, three-cylinder gas engine, the Smart Car can get better mileage than many hybrids, simply because it's small, round, and light. By far the most diminutive car on the American road, even the domestic model ranks number four, the highest nonhybrid, on the ACEEE list. At half the cost of

Find the "Green" Car. Recent models of the conventional and hybrid Honda Civic are virtually indistinguishable. Performance is hidden under the hood.

Smart Shape.
The original Smart Car, shown here in comparison to the MINI Cooper, the Prius, and the Hummer, gets better mileage than most hybrids, simply because of its size, shape, and weight.

a Prius, it outperforms many technology-driven vehicles—purely due to its shape and size. In India, the four-door Tata Nano gets 61 miles per gallon and costs the equivalent of $2,000, the price of a decent laptop computer. Tata's shapelier 2011 concept car, the Pixel, advertised as "the most package efficient four-seater in the world," boasts 69 miles per gallon and only 60 percent of standard emissions.

Imagine a day when we've perfectly solved the challenges of energy, resources, and emissions, and everything we do and make is clean, harmless, and infinitely renewable. Is that enough?

With all of these examples, the intelligence resides in the form, not the engine—in the visible design, not the invisible techniques. The lesson is that designers can get a lot smarter with low-tech solutions before jumping to high-tech systems. Design trumps technology.

High Tech and High Touch

The simple examples of the Tata and the Smart Car have broader implications for the shape of everything else. Smaller size means fewer raw materials, reduced volume, and less space to heat and cool. A standard American parking space can accommodate two Smart Cars end to end and almost four side by side. If everyone drove one, the widths of roads and areas of parking lots could shrink, along with the space in a garage and therefore the size of a house and the acreage of a lot. If everyone drove one, the geographic and environmental footprint of the entire built environment could shrink dramatically.

You might object that smaller cars aren't safe. Actually, despite its size, the Smart Car fares very well in safety tests, partly because of its rounded shape and compact frame, which the company compares to the structural integrity of a walnut. Fine, but tiny cars just aren't practical, you rebut. Tell that to the legions of European and Asian microcar drivers. Yes, but Americans are different, you say. That's true: the United Nations estimates that in the United States there are nearly eight vehicles per capita, the highest number in the world, and that the average American family owns at least two cars, the most common pairing being a full-sized pickup and a midsized sedan. A 2008 marketing study found that while the national average is 2.28 vehicles per household, the single largest group (35 percent) owns three or more. We do like our cars.

Yet, while the number of cars has gone up, the average number of occupants has gone down. Statistics for 2006 from the National Highway Traffic Safety Administration suggest an estimated 1.37 people per car per trip, and in many places the number is lower. Much of the time that we drive we're alone, so hauling around all the extra weight and volume of a larger car is unnecessary, expensive, and wasteful. Not every car needs four seats (although the Tata has them), and not every car needs to be big—or even midsized. For many of us, micro-vehicles are a more sensible choice. Logically speaking, smaller can be smarter, both environmentally and economically. So what's the hesitation?

The problem isn't logical, it's emotional—a matter for the heart, not the brain. We Americans prefer our cars bigger, like our houses and hamburgers. It's a cultural preference, and herein lies sustainability's most significant challenge—and its most fruitful opportunity. The supply of physical resources is one thing, but the demands of emotional predilections, born from years, lifetimes, and generations of custom and habit, are another. The key question is this: How do we align what we *crave* with what we *have*—or can or should

Small Is the New Big. *(a)* The 69-miles-per-gallon Tata Pixel concept car, "the most package efficient four-seater in the world," and *(b)* the 300-square-foot Wee House, by Alchemy Architects.

High Tech and High Touch.
(a) Joris Laarman's Bone Chair mimics
skeletal growth to put material only where
it's needed. *(b)* But in the many cultural
traditions, such as Japanese seiza, that prefer
sitting or kneeling on the floor, no chair at
all is needed.

have? The answer isn't to sacrifice our needs or urges; it's to satisfy them more gracefully by building health and wealth in more effective, fulfilling, and meaningful ways.

Environmental educator David Orr distinguishes between two kinds of sustainability. *Technological* sustainability is quantitative and relies on doing the same things more efficiently, whereas *ecological* sustainability is qualitative and requires a fundamentally new way of doing things. To explain the difference and demonstrate how both views are necessary, Orr gives a medical analogy. If a man suffers a heart attack, doctors must first return his vital signs to normal, just to keep him alive. But after his recovery comes the longer, slower process of dealing with deeper causes, such as diet, exercise, stress, relationships, and so forth. The green movement is still in the first stage—the earth is having a heart attack, and we're fumbling around for newfangled defibrillators. But we have yet to face the underlying social and cultural circumstances that brought about the heart attack.

The distinction may be thought of as one between *life support* and *lifestyle*. Imagine a day when we've perfectly solved the challenges of energy, resources, and emissions, and everything we do and make is clean, harmless, and infinitely renewable. Is that enough? Let's make it more personal: If you could take care of all your daily nutritional needs by ingesting one tasteless capsule, would you be satisfied? Would you miss the sweet scent of basil simmering in olive oil, or the way the nectar from a perfect peach cradles your tongue? You can merely deposit calories in your body, or you can savor their flavor. There's a world of difference between a vitamin C tablet and a glass of fresh-squeezed juice from a tree-ripened orange, and somewhere in that world lies the line between food and fuel, subsistence and sustenance, thriving and just surviving. Does sustaining life mean just maintaining a pulse, or does it also mean embracing all the things that make life worth living? Life is more than its "resources," and sustainable design must mean more than just the efficient use of those resources.

Futurist John Naisbitt writes that technology has accelerated rapidly while social change has not kept up: "At its best, technology supports and improves human life; at its worst, it alienates, isolates, distorts, and destroys." The more we depend on technology, the more we need to offset it with what Naisbitt calls "human ballast." He proposes two kinds of relationships—*High Tech* and *High*

Touch. "High Tech is about the demand on the individual to produce more in less time. High Touch is about process, about allowing time for discovery. . . . It is knowing when to unplug and when to plug in." One difference between Europeans and Americans is that Europeans drink their coffee from tiny cups while sitting still.

As sustainable design progresses, it will require and discover more High Tech strategies, but it will also need—desperately need—more High Touch solutions. The environmental crisis was instigated in part by conventional technology, and combating it with alternative technology can be a successful tactic—fighting fire with fire. But the proliferation of green tech demands more "human ballasts," and design can help strike the balance.

Sustainability and Sensuality

For such a familiar term, *sustainability* remains a surprisingly elusive and inconsistent concept. One simple description of its aim is *the harmony of nature and culture.* We tend to discuss these terms as binary, black-and-white conditions rather than as a spectrum of subtle gradations linking human and non-human life. Some argue that culture doesn't exist separately from nature, that everything human is as natural as everything else, while others contend that nature no longer exists, having been subsumed by human activity. In *The Wooing of Earth,* microbiologist René Dubos tries to resolve the argument by declaring that "humankind is *in* Nature but no longer quite *of* Nature." Humanity and the rest of life are overlapping spheres, and it is the degree of overlap that causes some debate. If they are completely separate, they don't overlap at all; if there is no distinction between the two, they merge; and there are many gradations between these two extremes. Regardless, the question is not necessarily the amount of overlap—it's the character of the connection. This, in essence, is ecology.

The textbook definition of *ecology* is "the study of the relationships and interactions between living organisms and their natural or developed environment." From this description, three important traits become clear: (1) ecology pertains to relationships, not just things; (2) those relationships are between the organisms themselves and between the organisms and their environment; and (3) the environment includes both the "natural" and "developed" worlds. Ecology encompasses the total environment and all of its associations. Ecological design, then, should work not just to preserve the natural environment of wildlife and watersheds; it should embrace the entire cultural environment as well.

So, sustainability relates to both nature and culture, but how important are aesthetics within each of the spheres? First, creative activity and artistic expression are the most evident earmarks of culture. Decoration, ornament, and art have appeared in every culture since the dawn of civilization—even before. Prior to the past decade, it was generally thought that the earliest art occurred in Europe some thirty-five thousand years ago, but in 2001, excavations at the southernmost tip of South Africa unearthed pieces of ochre rock ornamented with carved geometric patterns. Seventy thousand years old, these objects are not just the first abstract art—they're the oldest known examples of symbolic expression. The behavior that characterizes modern culture did not begin in Europe after people migrated out of Africa; it began much earlier, closer to the dawn of humanity. Anthropologists believe that the universality of artistic behavior, its spontaneous appearance throughout time across the globe, and the fact that it can be recognized across cultures all suggest that art stems from innate needs and desires. Aesthetic expression and appreciation are inherent to our species.

What of nature? Traditional ecologists trace the flow of *energy* through an ecosystem, but the emerging field of sensory ecology insists that the flow of *information* is essential. Sensory ecology studies how living things acquire and use information through sight, sound, scent, and the other senses in order to adapt and survive. Animals need information to maintain and navigate their environments and to communicate with one other. Recognizing and reacting to a potential mate or a possible threat, friend or foe, can mean the difference between life and death. Sensory experience and information are not just relevant to ecology—they are vital to it.

Look at birds. The brilliant plumage of the peacock and any number of tropical species attracts mates like a beacon. The male bower bird builds elaborate nests and decorates them with colorfully arranged fruits, nuts, and bobbles to get the attention of the female. "Amorous architecture," it's been called. Perhaps the most arresting example of sensory ecology is birdsong. Different species use pitch, melody, and rhythm to distinguish themselves in the concert hall of the forest. Birds can spread across large areas, and sound is the perfect medium to communicate over distances. The kakapo of New Zealand tramples a bowl into the earth to amplify its cry, which can be heard from four miles away. The nightingale has three hundred love songs in its repertoire, and the cowbird uses forty different notes, some too high for the human ear. But this symphony isn't just for the birds. Chirping actually can stimulate trees to open their stomata, the tiny pores on the underside of leaves that let out oxygen and take in carbon dioxide, moisture, and minerals. Birdsong helps clean the air and cultivate life.

Aesthetics are fundamental to both culture and nature, and if sustainability refers to the graceful interaction between them, it must have a sensory dimension. But how does this claim hold up against other definitions of sustainability? Undoubtedly, the one most frequently quoted comes from the 1987 United Nations study *Our Common Future,* also known as the "Brundtland Report." Over the past quarter century, the paraphrase of a single line has become a mantra for many environmentalists and designers alike: "meeting the needs of the present without compromising the ability of future generations to meet their needs." Many take this to mean we cannot squander current resources and leave nothing for our heirs. In his oft-cited 1992 address to the United Nations, Native American leader Oren Lyons urged societies "to make every decision on behalf of the seventh generation to come; to have compassion and love for those generations yet unborn."

These are very broad ambitions, much broader than the conservation of resources. The Brundtland definition is invariably taken out of context and rarely, if ever, discussed in terms of its social and cultural implications, though the report itself focused on global community and human fulfillment in relation to the earth's capacity, as another passage makes clear: "Sustainable development requires meeting the basic needs of all and extending to all the opportunity to fulfill their aspirations for a better life." Brundtland intends everyone to have the opportunity not merely to subsist but also to pursue their ambitions, to live out their dreams.

> "Aesthetics is not a luxury, but a universal human desire."
>
> *—Virginia Postrel*

Nevertheless, common views of sustainability are not informed by the complete content of Brundtland but, rather, by the popular quotation cited above. If we focus exclusively on "meeting needs," what does that entail? In 1943, psychologist Abraham Maslow famously described human motivation as a hierarchy of needs, ranging from physiological necessities to safety, belonging, esteem, and happiness. Usually presented as a pyramid with physical survival at the bottom, this hierarchy suggests that we pursue pleasure and emotional fulfillment only after ensuring our survival and security. If basic human necessities are stacked in such simple echelons, how far up the ladder should we climb before we can claim that "the needs of the present" have been met? Are food and water enough, or should we include safety and security? What about friendship and family?

Life isn't this straightforward. In nature, needs do not conform to a neat list of priorities; sensory urges compel most creatures to satisfy their hunger, thirst, and sexual longings. People are the same, for many of our most visceral experiences begin with the drive to survive. The mouth waters with the smell of food cooking, the blood stirs with the sight of a sexual partner, and adrenaline jumps at sudden noises. Maslow's pyramid dissolves in a swirling cauldron where need and desire continually roil. Without sensory attraction, not only would life be less fulfilling—it would cease to exist.

"Human beings do not wait for aesthetics until they have full stomachs and a roof that doesn't leak," writes cultural observer Virginia Postrel. "They do not pursue aesthetic needs 'only when basic needs have been satisfied.' Given a modicum of stability and sustenance, people enrich the look and feel of their lives through ritual, personal adornment, and decorated objects." In a subsistence economy, she explains, better health or housing might be unaffordable or unattainable, whereas ornamentation not only doesn't require much expense but actually makes the absence of other amenities bearable. Art and design can feed the soul even when the body goes hungry. "Poor people create the body decoration that illustrates *National Geographic*. Poor people built the cathedrals of Europe and developed the sand paintings of Tibet. Poor people turned baskets and pottery into decorative art. Poor people invented paints and dyes, jewelry and cosmetics. . . . These artifacts do not reflect societies focused only on 'lower-order' needs. Aesthetics is not a luxury, but a universal human desire."

The most commonly cited definition of sustainability concerns the enduring effort to meet our basic needs, and nature inspires the meeting of those needs through the attainment of sensory pleasure. Desire is the engine of evolution. Sensual experience is embedded in the very idea of sustainability.

Beauty's Triple Bottom Line

Another popular definition of sustainability comes from business guru John Elkington, who in 1994 expanded the traditional notion of value to include not just economic but social and environmental measures as well—the "triple bottom line." Environmentalism is not a synonym for but, rather, a subset of sustainability. Some speak of the triple bottom line as a trade-off between the three values, whereas others consider the values mutually supportive, the whole being greater than the sum of the parts. Either way, I can think of nothing at all, certainly nothing of value, that doesn't fall within one or more of these categories. Even the most intangible human and natural treasures are social or environmental in origin, so the triple bottom line must include even the emotional and the spiritual—love, family, faith, and, yes, beauty.

Aesthetics can shore up all three pillars of people, profit, and planet, even if conventional wisdom disagrees. Ever since Plato ruminated on shadows in caves, we have been told that images are illusory, that looks can be deceiving. But, as Postrel writes in *The Substance of Style,* distrust of appearances is puritanical prejudice: "The preachers—secular and religious, contemporary and historical—tell us that surfaces are meaningless, misleading distractions of no genuine value. But our experience and intuition suggest otherwise. Viscerally, if not intellectually, we're convinced that style does matter, that look and feel add something important to our lives. . . . We judge people, places, and things at least in part by how they look. We care about surfaces."

Popular designer Karim Rashid agrees: "Every business should be completely concerned with beauty. It is after all a collective human need." In the past decade or so, manufacturers in every industry have learned the economic value of aesthetics. Apple singlehandedly incited design revolutions with the iMac, the iPod, and the iPhone. The candy-colored iMacs, the first to signal that computers need not be drab beige, sent Apple's sales through the roof, and profits doubled after the iPad tablet hit the market in early 2010. In the mid-1990s, Motorola released a newly designed version of a popular pager device. Little had changed, except the new model was a bright, translucent green instead of basic black, but it sold big—and at a higher price. "All the fancy-ass technological engineering in the world couldn't get us a nickel more for the products," Iain Morris, Motorola's pager division head at the time, told Postrel. "But squirt-gun green plastic, which actually cost us nothing, could get us fifteen bucks extra per unit." Looks sell.

In fact, in today's economy, looks might be the chief commodity. As Richard Lanham explains in *The Economics of Attention,* we reportedly live in an "information economy," but economists study the allocation of scarce resources, and information isn't in short supply. With some 100 million Web sites, a couple million television shows on thousands of networks, and half a million new books published every year in English alone, there's an enormous flow of information, all available 24/7. What's scarce is the ability to make sense of it all—to sort, absorb, and digest it. How do you sip from a fire hose?

"Beauty is the promise of happiness."

—*Stendahl*

In such an economy, the most precious resource, claims Lanham, is human attention, and what regulates attention is *style.* "Attracting attention is what style is all about," Lanham writes. "If attention is now at the center of the economy, rather than stuff, then so is style. It moves from the periphery to the center. Style and substance trade places." In an economy of stuff, science and technology rule, but in an economy of style, arts and humanities take over. "They are the disciplines that study how attention is allocated, how cultural capital is created and traded." Aesthetics and design represent the most potentially valuable economic mechanisms today.

Tourism, driven in large part by sightseeing, represents 30 percent of the world's annual commercial service exports. People flock to places with scenic beauty, architectural character, and aesthetic distinction, which is why the Swiss government pays dairy farmers to keep their cows visible in the pastures. The marketing research company FutureBrand tracks how icons of architecture and nature spur tourism; Angkor Wat in Cambodia, Mount Kilimanjaro in Tanzania, and the kangaroo in Australia all generate positive associations and visitation, because people are drawn to compelling images even if they don't actually witness them firsthand. How many visitors Down Under actually commune with koalas?

One exciting building can jump-start a whole economy. Before the Guggenheim Museum was built there in 1997, Bilbao, Spain, was a modest and admittedly unattractive industrial town. Then, over the following decade, 9 million visitors came, and, according to CNN, more than 80 percent of the city's tourists say they venture there specifically to see that single sight. The *Financial Times* estimated that in the first three years the museum generated 500 million Euros in economic activity—and 100 million in taxes. The so-called Bilbao Effect isn't exclusive to Bilbao. After the iconic Seattle Public Library opened in 2004, attendance tripled and profit margins for neighboring businesses rose 50 percent. One merchant told a local newspaper, "It's a bit like having Disneyland across the street."

Aesthetics influence not just prosperity but also well-being—both wealth and welfare. "Beauty is the promise of happiness," wrote Stendahl, and evidence backs this up. In *Who's Your City?* (2008), Richard Florida shows that where you live, more than any other single factor, determines whether you're happy. After polling nearly thirty thousand people in a "Place and Happiness Survey," co-conducted with the Gallup Organization, Florida found that of the five criteria affecting happiness, the top of the list was aesthetics: the higher people rate the appearance of their community, the higher their overall level of satisfaction. Florida calls it "the beauty premium."

In their landmark 2004 study, *Cities Ranked & Rated*, Bert Sperling and Peter Sander came to the same conclusion. Evaluating four hundred North

American cities with various criteria affecting "livability," they singled out "physical attractiveness," because how good a place looks can influence both initial impressions and long-term satisfaction. "The effects of a pancake-flat, windswept, nondescript landscape with dirty air and little vegetation are far different from that of attractive, well-kept, tree-lined streets with good buildings and pristine mountain, valley river, or lake-side setting."

All this research points to a simple fact—people are better off in places that are attractive, richly landscaped, and intimately connected to their natural settings. Other studies show that we also take better care of such environments, which tend to have less litter, waste, and vandalism. The "Broken Windows" theory proposes that a disorderly environment encourages vandalism and other crimes by signaling that the environment isn't meant to be respected; visible disrepair creates a slippery slope of abuse. This logic is widely believed to explain the dramatic drop in crime in New York in the early 1990s, after the city started a program to keep the subways free of graffiti, the most common type of vandalism. A 2005 Harvard study showed that keeping a neighborhood clean can reduce crime by 20 percent. Graffiti occurs most in areas that are already visibly neglected, particularly on large walls with smooth, drab, unbroken surfaces, so ugly buildings are tempting canvases. On the other hand, textured, finely detailed, and colorful walls, as well as vegetation, discourage defacement. What's attractive to the eye is less attractive to the vandal.

A 2008 Dutch report indicates that preventing graffiti also can more than halve the incidence of littering, a persistent environmental challenge. The American Public Works Association (APWA) defines litter as "material which, if thrown or deposited, tends to create a danger to public health, safety and welfare." Litter is stuff that in itself isn't inherently bad; it's stuff that becomes bad—environmentally, socially, aesthetically—when left where it doesn't belong. "There's no such thing as waste," declares Berkeley professor of design Galen Cranz. "There's only material out of place." Litter is the first visual cue of material out of place. According to the APWA, the greatest volume of it—up to 60 percent—consists of beverage containers, which typically break down very slowly. Aluminum cans take up to a century to biodegrade, glass bottles a million years, and plastic bottles—well, most of them never do. So the majority of litter could linger in perpetuity, cluttering up the corners of the world, forever out of place.

The impact on the triple bottom line is enormous: cleanup costs $11.5 billion annually, quality of life visibly suffers, with increased crime and declining property values, and all that trash ends up clogging waterways and choking ecosystems. Roadways are particularly vulnerable. The social and spatial isolation of spending much of our time in cars can exaggerate one of the leading causes of litter, a sense of entitlement that psychologists describe as alienation from the environment. According to the Federal Highway Administration, every year over 51 billion pieces of litter line U.S. roads—that's nearly seven thousand items per mile, so you're not likely to drive a single foot without seeing trash.

By contrast, people tend to litter less and even pick up after one another in outdoor recreational areas such as parks and campgrounds—places with more vegetation. The same is true of urban areas, so denser, pedestrian-friendly, heavily planted neighborhoods—those generally described as more attractive—also promote environmental protection. Finally, the amount of litter drops noticeably if waste receptacles are conspicuous and attractively designed. If "litter begets litter," as the saying goes, then a tidy world inspires a tidier world. A respectable-looking place commands respect.

This is why the Keep America Beautiful campaign focuses on visual attraction as the cornerstone of conservation. "Beauty is a silent but powerful force that makes communities safer, healthier and more livable," the Web site proclaims. "America's cities and towns are being transformed by visionary community leaders who recognize the value of beautification to attract residents, draw tourism, sustain economies, and repel the elements of blight and decay." Conservation and comfort both relate to visual quality because attraction instills both respect and well-being. A gorgeous environment is a greener environment.

Redefining Style

Nevertheless, aesthetics are, as Florida points out, "under-appreciated." Beauty gets a bad rap, for people often consider it luxurious at best, superficial at least, and harmful at worst. In 2010, the Australian government mandated unembellished cigarette packaging for fear of attractive graphics distracting from the warning labels. A more common view is that beauty can be shallow, false, or fleeting. In a disposable world, writes design critic Karrie Jacobs, "style is the most disposable thing there is." Yet, the word itself (from *stylus,* or "pen") refers literally to a way of doing things (such as a flare with handwriting), and green is nothing if not a reconsideration of how we do things. Style should matter.

Unfortunately, the most familiar attempts to bring style to sustainability have become aesthetic clichés. Hemp shirts, rattan furniture, unbleached paper, wood-pulp walls, and wheat-board cabinets suggest that "earth-friendly" should look earthy. "Eco-fashion conjures up images of burlap sacks," *Forbes* magazine announced in 2010. Structures built from scrap metal or shipping containers, chairs made from traffic signs, and dresses fashioned out of plastic bags all wear their discarded parts on their sleeves. Solar panels and grass roofs have become a staple of green buildings, but when reduced to a conspicuous appliqué they become what some architects call "green bling."

Associating sustainability with its trappings rather than its principles risks looking passé. Has the planted roof become the environmentalist equivalent of the Chia Pet? Rising interest in green brings more ingenuity from designers, and many recent examples have shown that sustainability can be attractive. But in much of this work, decisions about shape and appearance are driven by a different standard—namely, the designer's personal preferences—than are decisions about technique. Some examples ignore aesthetics, and some apply it superficially. Neither is enough.

Sustainability should *have* style but not become *a* style. What designers need isn't an ecological aesthetic—it's an aesthetics of ecology, a set of principles and mechanics for making design more responsive and responsible, environmentally, socially, and economically. The Smart Car, Tata's Nano and Pixel, and the Kamm-tail Prius show how the very concept of a design—in these cases, the size and shape—can enhance sustainability. Similarly, Yves Béhar's Mission One electric motorcycle capitalizes on the lack of a gas engine by indenting the sides so the rider can pull her legs out of the slipstream, creating a much more aerodynamic form. With the change in technology came a change in shape—and in the results. What makes these cases environmentally intelligent is precisely what makes them visually distinctive. They demonstrate a direct relationship between form and performance and show that shape itself can aid sustainability.

At the outset of the 1970s energy crisis, economist E. F. Schumacher wrote: "Ever bigger machines, entailing ever bigger concentrations of economic power and exerting ever greater violence against the environment, do not represent progress: they are a denial of wisdom. Wisdom demands a new orientation of science and technology towards the organic, the gentle, the non-violent, the elegant and beautiful." Four decades later, the design industry has begun successfully to orient science and technology toward the organic and the "gentle" by establishing popular standards for a less violent impact on the earth, but it has yet to outline a clear concept and practical approach for the elegant and the beautiful.

The next chapter attempts to do just that.

CONSERVATION.

Ecofont. Studying how much of a letter can be removed and still be readable, the designers introduced tiny holes in the characters to cut ink usage by 25 percent.

ATTRACTION.

Meeker & Associates, ClearviewHWY. Taller letters, more open shapes, and better spacing improve the legibility of road signs while reducing the effects of glare for older and visually impaired drivers.

CONNECTION.

Allessio Leonardi, BMF Change. Designed in 2008 as the official font of the city of Berlin, it enhances community identity through an image the creators call "confident" and "stocky," embodying the "sturdy" character of the city.

ecofont

Bergaults

be open
be free
be berlin

The Three Principles Applied to
Typeface Design

3 | Three Principles

Nothing is quite beautiful alone.

—Ralph Waldo Emerson

"WHEN I AM WORKING ON A PROBLEM, I never think about beauty," claimed legendary designer Buckminster Fuller. "I only think about how to solve the problem. But when I have finished, if the solution is not beautiful, I know it is wrong." Fuller, inventor of the geodesic dome and famed for his rationality, understood that beauty is essential, but he evidently had no process for creating it that rivaled his logical approach to everything else. Does beauty result only from trial and error, or can it be produced more methodically, as part of the "problem" to be solved?

In 2009, Gary Hamel, named the world's most influential business thinker by the *Wall Street Journal*, proclaimed that good design is like the Supreme

Court's view of pornography: "We know it when we see it." Professionals and the public alike speak of art, design, and beauty as veiled in mystery, as if inspiration has divine origins, a gift from the muses. Novelist D. H. Lawrence rhapsodized about his own inspiration: "Not I, not I, but the wind that blows through me." Feeding this impression is an elitist idea that great artists and designers have some special or privileged viewpoint that goes beyond thorough training and hard work, as if angels whisper secrets in their ears that others can't hear.

Biologist E. O. Wilson rejects the romanticizing of creativity: "The arts are not solely shaped by errant genius out of historical circumstances and idiosyncratic personal experience. The roots of their inspiration date back in deep history to the genetic origins of the human brain, and are permanent." Inspiration and innovation are not the exclusive territory of a select group of souls with sacred gifts bestowed from on high. Competent professionals in any field can create things of great sensitivity and elegance by becoming smarter about the practice of their crafts.

Yet, it is a mistake—possibly the most tragic mistake of modern design— to believe that the burden of time and devotion falls to the individual alone. The igloo wasn't invented by one really smart "Eskimo"—it is a testament to the resourcefulness and grace of the entire Inuit people, living their land and accumulating wisdom for untold generations. The design profession attempts to impart encyclopedic knowledge and centuries of tradition through relatively few years of education and training, and we wonder why there is so much bad design. Designers' customs, habits, and standards are seriously inadequate to take on the challenge of sustainability. "We cannot solve our problems with the same thinking we used when we created them," Einstein declared. We need new ways of thinking about design.

In the 1950s, scientist and novelist C. P. Snow claimed that in the modern era many of the world's problems stemmed from the division of thought into separate sensibilities—"the two cultures" of the arts and sciences. Today, contends Wilson, this chasm is at the heart of the environmental crisis: "Until that fundamental divide is closed or at least reconciled in some congenial manner, the relation between man and the living world will remain problematic." In *Consilience: The Unity of Knowledge,* Wilson champions this "new frontier," the bridge between intelligence and intuition. Science, he avows, does not "imprison the spark of artistic genius"; in fact, the scientific method can enhance and improve creativity. Certainly no field can learn more from this new unity than design, which already is a kind of art-science.

Never before have the shapers of things had greater need for wisdom and innovation.

To develop the art and science of a more natural design, we can look to nature itself and discover what shapes it. For example, Saguaro cacti, the majestic "sentinels of the desert," can grow up to fifty feet and live two hundred years. The fluting of the column helps the saguaro stand tall but also allows it to expand like an accordion during the wet season and shrink during the dry. Its lovely bell-shaped blossoms cradle sweet nectar that lures in pollinating bats and insects. The flowers open in the evening to reveal an ochre interior attractive to bees, who see the world in yellow. The saguaro grows only in the very specific environment of the Sonoran Desert, especially southern Arizona. Farther north is too cold; farther south, too hot. A slight difference in latitude could not have produced these incredible creatures.

The saguaro suggests three principles that drive the aesthetics of ecology: shape for efficiency, shape for pleasure, and shape for place. These three values—*conservation, attraction,* and *connection*—can guide designers to make things more environmentally intelligent, humane, and elegant all at once.

Conservation: Shape for Efficiency

"Beauty rests on necessities," wrote Emerson. "The line of beauty is the result of perfect economy. The cell of the bee is built at that angle which gives the most strength with the least wax. The bone in the quill of the bird gives the most alar strength with the least weight. . . . There is not a particle to spare in natural structures." The philosopher equates beauty with elegant economy, also a pretty good description of sustainability. The "3 Rs" of conservation—Reduce, Reuse, Recycle—are familiar even to schoolchildren. Yet, while the three are listed in order of priority, with recycling as a last resort, the latter has taken over as the most prominent policy, as if to minimize the impact on personal lifestyles: instead of tossing something in the trash can, we toss it in a sorting bin. Design needs new strategies for reduction prior to the consumer stage. The first step is a fourth "R"—*Rethink.*

The public dialogue about climate change centers on renewable resources—where and how we get energy and materials—but this is only half the challenge. How we *use* them is just as important as how we source them. According to the International Energy Agency, the percentage of energy usage that comes from

oil and gas is higher now than it was in 1973. Even if per capita consumption flattens, rising population will continue to increase the totals. To make a dent in total consumption, we have to become dramatically more efficient.

Sometimes called the "sixth fuel" (after coal, oil, gas, nuclear, and renewables), energy efficiency may itself be considered a source of power—by some estimations the single largest source, yet one that remains comparatively untapped in design. The most familiar methods of improving efficiency are better materials, such as improved insulation in buildings, and better equipment, such as low-heat motors; yet, often, these mechanical gains merely offset losses brought about by poor planning—good tactics compensating for bad strategy.

But design can make great strides to ensure smart consumption as well as smart production. "Most commercial buildings today could be built with half the materials," designer Neri Oxman said when accepting the 2009 Earth Award. "We could save 6 million metric tons of CO_2 for the life of the building." Alternative energy is essential; alternative design, more so. Ironically, one of the clearest statements about the importance of strategic design comes from an industrial tycoon arguably responsible for many of the habits that led to the environmental crisis: "It is not possible to repeat too often that waste is not something which comes after the fact," proclaimed Henry Ford in 1924. "Picking up and reclaiming scrap left over after production is a public service, but planning so that there will be no scrap is a higher public service." Planning for zero waste serves the public. Buckminster Fuller translated this into a simple equation: "Efficiency = doing more with less."

Industrial designer Guy Robinson names three chief goals for sustainable design: "put less stuff in a product," "create products that use less stuff," and "create fewer products." The most obvious way to "use less stuff" is to make things smaller, and the Tata Nano and the Smart Car illustrate just how smart small can be. In 2009, Kellogg introduced a space-saving cereal box that is shorter and wider than the traditional eight- by eleven-inch box but holds the same volume with less packaging. The new compact form also fits on shelves more efficiently, putting more units in the same space. With one simple change in shape, the Corn Flakes box cuts material, saves room, and displays more merchandise, which could boost sales.

Buildings can learn from cereal boxes. Many insist that a structure's size is the single most important factor in its consumption, and in recent years there has been a veritable onslaught of tiny eco-homes, such as the 300-square-foot Wee House, the architectural equivalent of the Nano and a striking antidote to the bloated McMansions populating suburban America. The size of the average house has more than doubled in the past half century, while the size of the average household has dropped by 25 percent in the same time period, according to the U.S. Census Bureau. Recently, however, the trend began reversing. According to *USA Today*, in a single quarter during 2008, the average area of new single-family homes shrank by more than 10 percent, and 90 percent of builders surveyed by the National Association of Home Builders in 2009 said they planned to build smaller, more affordable houses. A 2010 survey by the real estate watcher Trulia.com found that only 9 percent of respondents prefer homes over 3,200 square feet, while more than a third said their ideal size was under 2,000 feet. "The McMansion Era Is Over," Trulia announced. Small is the new big.

Yet, downsizing homes won't work unless they offer more to homeowners. "Everybody hates the Calvinist sacrifice; they just don't want to hear of it," architect and planner Andrés Duany told the *New York Times* in 2010. McMansions have served a perverse purpose, he argues, by attempting to replace amenities that had disappeared from public life—an exercise room substitutes for a park, a home theater for the Main Street cinema, the great room for the town square. Going small can succeed only if these missing pieces of the townscape reappear. Shrunken structures must accompany more active communities, and, conversely, building smaller might actually encourage more social interaction—and healthier lifestyles—by nudging people out into public space. Smaller has to be better for the planet and for people at the same time.

Fuller's concept of "ephemeralization" predicts that the greater a product's sophistication, the smaller it gets. Consider the evolution of the computer from the size of a building to the size of a room to a desktop, laptop, and handheld. The Consumer Electronics Association's 2008 report on sustainability emphasizes miniaturization: "As cell phones, computers, cameras, and nearly every other product become smaller and lighter for easier portability, so too do their environmental footprints shrink. Smaller products require fewer raw materials." Yes and no. Many things are fabricated from materials with standardized sizes and shapes, such as two-by-fours, four-by-eight plywood, and I-beams in buildings, and if a design doesn't conform to these manufactured dimensions, the bits and pieces left over can get discarded. Using prefabricated parts requires working with their dimensions (known as "modular design").

Furthermore, the resources needed to manufacture high-tech products can be enormous, regardless of their size. Apple's paper-thin MacBook Air,

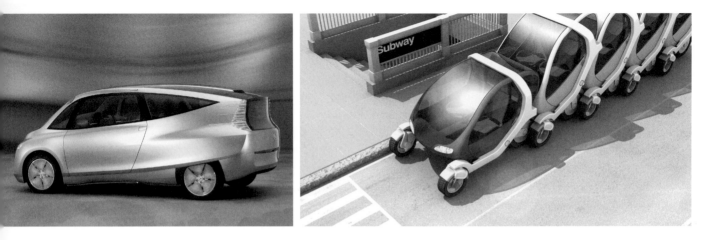

Shape for Efficiency. *(a)* DaimlerChrysler's DCX "Bionic" car emulates the form of the highly streamlined boxfish to get 84 miles per gallon. *(b)* MIT Media Lab's five-foot-long electric CityCars stack up like grocery carts to fit five hundred on a typical city block—six times more than standard cars.

introduced in 2008, is gorgeously sleek, like an aluminum placemat. *Thinnovation*, they call it. Apple has called the MacBook Air the "greenest" laptop available, comparing its emissions over four years to that of a car in a single month. Sounds great, but the Air is two thousand times lighter than a car—2.5 pounds versus 2.5 tons. Per unit weight of material, its emissions exceed those of an automobile by a factor of forty. Is a Mustang greener than a Mac?

Different scales of things can behave differently. A rose is no more natural than a redwood; a minnow, no more than a whale. Efficiency takes more than merely making the same design smaller. Don't just minimize size; optimize shape—think before shrink. The Creative Edge Design Group transformed the standard bulbous milk carton into an interlocking squared shape with the same volume, but, because it stacks without crates, it can store 50 percent more milk in a cubic foot. The automotive equivalents are the MIT Media Lab's five-foot-long electric CityCars, which, when parked, stack like grocery carts to fit five hundred cars on a city block instead of the usual eighty.

As any fitness or martial arts expert will tell you, power comes from form, not bulk, and design is the same. Of his cardboard bridge over France's Gardon River, architect Shigeru Ban says: "The strength and durability of a structure have nothing to do with the material." In Fuller's words: "Efficiency makes it mandatory that we USE forces, not FIGHT them." Going with the flow is how fish maneuver in rough water; by curving their bodies around eddies in the current, they can propel forward with very little energy. Speed comes from the shape of the movement, not just the strength of the muscle. DaimlerChrysler's

DCX "Bionic" concept car, inspired by the form of the highly streamlined box-fish, can get up to 84 miles per gallon—with a diesel engine.

Streamlining is not just for race cars and jet planes. Overcoming air drag takes more than half the power required for a car to cruise at highway speeds. "The main driver for lower aerodynamic drag is fuel economy," according to Max Schenkel of General Motors. "As long as federal standards for fuel economy increase and fuel costs go up, aerodynamic drag will have to be improved." At the moment, most vehicles on the road are boxy sedans, SUVs, and trucks, but in 2011, U.S. automakers agreed to achieve a national average fuel economy of 54.5 miles per gallon by 2025; this will force more ingenuity in how cars are shaped, not just how they're powered.

Better design doesn't have to break the bank. "Aero benefits can almost be cost-free to some extent—just how you bend the metal and how you execute gaps and joints," says Chrysler's Rick Aneiros. "If you're trying to reduce weight by adding expensive exotic materials, that's not easy to do. And improving engine efficiency, that's not easy to do. So the leading strategy is to improve aerodynamics whenever possible." The company SkinzWraps invented a dimpled car-body cover that improves fuel economy by 20 percent. Like golf balls and shark skin, the finely grained face creates tiny eddies of current that counteract drag. The new electric Aptera 2, marketed as "the most aerodynamically efficient vehicle ever," has only a third of the wind drag of a typical sedan and looks more like a plane than a car. "If a plane looked like an SUV, it wouldn't take off," says Bill Gross, Aptera's founder. "Dolphins don't look like SUVS for a reason. Cars need to look like dolphins, not SUVs."

> "Cars need to look like dolphins, not SUVs."
> —*Bill Gross*

As design becomes more sophisticated, more than just automobiles will behave like dolphins. "Evolution tends toward the accelerated developments of new form," said Fuller, and this is evident in every scale of design, from consumer products to buildings and cities, and in every circumstance, from the everyday to the exotic, from the simple to the spectacular. PAX Scientific's Lily Impeller rotor mimics the logarithmic spiral of seashells and other natural forms to reduce energy by 85 percent. Eiji Nakatsu reshaped the nose of the sonic boom–prone Shinkansen bullet train to emulate the kingfisher's beak, which can penetrate water with surprisingly little splash. The sleeker, quieter train moves 10 percent

Twisted Tower.
Gensler, Shanghai Tower.
The 120-degree torque dramatically cuts wind loads, and therefore the amount of steel, by 25 percent, saving $60 million. The tall building was born well over a century ago. Why did it take architects so long to streamline it?

faster with 15 percent less energy. After studying the tubercles, or serrations, on humpback whale flippers, the aptly named Frank Fish developed a similar wind-turbine blade that moves at lower speeds, with 40 percent greater efficiency.

Even the most ordinary products can show great ingenuity. The rippled egg crate of the EcoGrip coffee cup sleeve uses air instead of material as an insulator, saving up to half the paper of other sleeves while presenting a more tactile surface to grasp. Glad's new striated trash bags have more strength with less material, annually saving 6.5 million pounds of plastic, or 140 million extra bags. Tiny holes in the Ecofont typeface cut ink usage by 25 percent—pointillist printing. The "diverging diamond" roadway interchange reroutes traffic in a braided pattern to alleviate congestion, take up less land, and slash the number of accidents in half.

To study the possibilities for buildings, the National Renewable Energy Laboratory conducted three thousand simulations and found that fully optimizing design can achieve up to a 60 percent energy savings on average—at no extra cost. The 120-degree twist of the Shanghai Tower redirects wind loads to flow around its face, cutting the amount of necessary steel by 25 percent and saving $60 million. The London City Hall shades itself by leaning into the sun, saving up to three-quarters of the energy used by a typical office building. The sculpted bullet shape of China's Pearl River Tower channels wind through turbines located in two horizontal slots in the building, cutting energy use by 60 percent. The diaphanous south facade of the San Francisco Federal Building provides enough shading to eliminate two-thirds of the mechanical system. The same architects' curvaceous new Phare Tower in Paris applies the idea to every aspect of the design, from form to detail. Says Thom Mayne, the chief designer: "When you start changing the shape, you start really changing the behavior of buildings."

Attraction: Shape for Pleasure

"A thing of beauty is a joy for ever," declared Keats. It's one thing for a poet to claim this, but an economist? In *Small Is Beautiful: Economics as if People Mattered,* E. F. Schumacher writes that the modern economist "is used to measuring the 'standard of living' by the amount of annual consumption, assuming all the time that a man who consumes more is 'better off' than a man who consumes less. A Buddhist economist would consider this approach excessively irrational:

since consumption is merely a means to human well-being, the aim should be to obtain the maximum of well-being with the minimum of consumption." In other words, conservation alone is not enough. We can get rid of waste while growing welfare—make the planet healthier and people happier.

Happiness sounds difficult to define, much less measure, but this is exactly what the New Economics Foundation does. Their Happy Planet Index (HPI) uses three indicators—environmental footprint, life satisfaction, and life expectancy—to measure mathematically "the ecological efficiency with which human well-being is delivered." This groundbreaking method pins down the elusive connections between quantity and quality—stuff and life—and puts real numbers to Schumacher's goal of maximum well-being with minimum consumption. By this standard, in 2009 the "happiest" place on the planet was Costa Rica, which reports the highest life satisfaction in the world and the second-highest life expectancy in the Americas, after Canada. (The United States ranked 114th out of 178 in the HPI.) The same year, Yale University's Environmental Performance Index named Costa Rica the third "greenest" nation, after Iceland and Switzerland, and FutureBrand's annual Country Brand Index, which evaluates the strength of a region's image, called Costa Rica the second "most scenic" country, after Tahiti. One place topping all three lists suggests connections between beauty, happiness, and stewardship, but which is the chicken and which are the eggs?

$$\text{HAPPY PLANET INDEX} = \frac{\textbf{Quality of Life}}{\textbf{Ecological Footprint}}$$

The Measure of Pleasure.
The New Economics Foundation's Happy Planet Index compares indicators for a nation's life satisfaction and life expectancy with its environmental footprint to calculate mathematically "the ecological efficiency with which human well-being is delivered." Could a similar method be applied to cities, buildings, and even consumer products to create a *Happy Product Index*?

If feeling good in a gorgeous setting such as Costa Rica seems only natural, that's the point—beauty can influence how we feel and how we treat our surroundings. But what can design do for more commonplace conditions? What would an iconography of happiness look like, and how can it be measured? The HPI evaluates entire countries, places of various sizes defined artificially by political boundaries, but theoretically the same idea could apply at any scale—a region, a community, a neighborhood, even a building or a consumer product. With reliable measures for conservation, health, and satisfaction, a *Happy Product Index* could paint a clear picture of a "happy city," a "happy house," even a "happy sofa."

With user satisfaction involved, such an index certainly would include an aesthetic component. "To many an engineer's dismay, the appearance of a product, or the way it feels physically, can sometimes make or break the product's market reaction," write interaction designers Julie Khaslavsky and

Nathan Shedroff. The square milk jug mentioned earlier is more efficient, cheaper and easier to ship, better for the environment, and smarter for the milk, which remains fresher because it packs more easily and can get to the market more quickly. Yet, although both Wal-Mart and Costco began stocking it in 2008, it has yet to catch on widely. Why? "It spills everywhere," a Sam's Club customer told the *New York Times*. The compact but unorthodox shape has no real spout and can be cumbersome to use. "It's very hard for kids to pour," said a different customer, and another was more frank: "I hate it." When people hate something, they won't use it, no matter how super-efficient the design.

Automobile design legend J Mays tells the tale of the Audi A2, the engineering of which was first-rate—lightweight, highly fuel efficient, and arranged thoroughly for disassembly and recycling. Yet, because it wasn't considered attractive, it didn't sell—it played to people's environmental ethics but not to their emotions. Not so of the Mays-designed New Beetle. One of the most beloved cars to come out in decades, Volkswagen's "cartoon of a car in the best sense" is "unlike anything else on the road today," proclaimed the Auto Channel when the Beetle premiered in 1998. "It looks like the world's biggest radio-controlled toy. . . . Has Volkswagen invented a cure for road rage?" The opposite of rage, according to *Roget's*, is happiness.

Where design and delight intersect is what critic Ingrid Fetell calls the "aesthetics of joy." Design, she says, can foster a healthier culture of consumption, based on relationships between people and objects that are meaningful, rewarding, and "emotionally sustainable: pleasurable not just on the first encounter, but for the long term." Joy is a renewable resource: "Like bamboo or sunlight, it will never run out." What designs that last have in common, say Khaslavsky and Shedroff, is "the ability to create an emotional bond with their audiences, almost a need for them," and they outline a three-part process for forming and keeping this bond: *Enticement* (grab attention), *Relationship* (make progress gradually), and *Fulfillment* (deliver the goods). Novelty might accomplish the first step but won't prolong our interest, which a product does chiefly through quality—"the feel of a fabric, the fit of a garment, the strength of a handle."

In 2010, when Apple launched the iPad, its first tablet computer, novelist and actor Stephen Fry wrote in *Time* magazine that "one doesn't relate to it as a 'tool'; the experience is closer to one's relationship with a person or an animal." Products are not merely a sum of their features, he explains: "We are human beings; our first responses to anything are dominated not by calculations but by feelings. . . . If you have an object in your pocket or hand for hours every day, then your relationship with it is profound, human and emotional. Apple's success has been founded on consumer products that address this side of us: their products make users smile as they reach forward to manipulate, touch, fondle, slide, tweak, pinch, prod and stroke."

The beauty of Apple's products, Fry believes, stems from their ability to "make users smile," and it has been suggested to me that somehow counting the number of grins a product provokes might be one way to measure its capacity to promote pleasure. The Auto Channel hinted at this method in its Volkswagen review: "The New Beetle generates more smiles per mile than anything on wheels." Four years later, the *New York Times* claimed the same of the MINI Cooper: "It is fair to say that almost no new vehicle in recent memory has provoked more smiles."

This is playful speculation, of course, but could smiles be tallied accurately? Facial recognition software can track the slightest change in expression and discern someone's mood, and retailers already use "videomining"— computer analysis of in-store videos—to understand shoppers' habits and determine whether people like or dislike a product. In other words, computers can count smiles. At the moment, the technique is used only to sell more merchandise, but it could be adapted as a design tool to help create products and places people are more likely to enjoy.

Cognitive scientist and design critic Donald Norman routinely uses the smile factor as a measure of success. He observes that products such as Phillipe Starck's insectile "Juicy Salif" citrus juicer or the toy-like Francis-Francis! Espresso maker often lead people to say, "It makes me smile," or "I want to touch it." The whimsy of objects such as Michael Graves's Rooster tea kettle can make us overlook their functional faults. Norman believes the grin-inducing boost in the morning could outweigh the fact that the kettle is awkward to use.

He might be right. The act of smiling releases serotonin, the "happy chemical" in the brain, relieving stress and promoting health. Smiling is infectious— we see others do it, and we involuntarily join in—which suggests that not just the act but also the very image is beneficial. Studies indicate that smiling makes you appear to others as more sincere, attractive, sociable, and competent. In 2009, electrical utility companies in ten major U.S. cities began putting smiley faces on the monthly statements of households using lower-than-average power, and it led to even more savings. A happy image—in this case, the simplest, most iconic of happy images—can encourage conservation, a fact some are calling "climate psychology." Can design that triggers a smile promote both better feelings and better behavior?

For sheer smile power, my Smart Car upstages the Beetle and the MINI. Everywhere I drive, people turn and beam (it's the *car*, I have to remind myself), so I like to think I'm spreading joy through the land. Strangers approach me in parking lots and say it reminds them of an automotive puppy, and they might be onto something. In the 1940s, animal behaviorist Konrad Lorenz argued that people respond affectionately to anything with baby-like features—round proportions, large heads, big eyes, and so forth. In 2009, biologists at the University of Pennsylvania discovered that looking at babies causes a chemical reaction deep in the brain. Cuteness is addictive, which explains why videos of infants, puppies, and kittens have received more than a billion hits online—and why strangers find my Smart Car irresistible.

Nevertheless, design critic Victor Papanek considered this exploitative: "Cuteness is the enemy of beauty." Apparently, however, it's not the enemy of productivity. A 2009 University of Virginia study found that viewing puppies and kittens actually improves task-oriented performance; "the tenderness elicited by something 'cute,'" the authors found, "is more than just a positive affective feeling state—it can literally make people more physically tender in their motor behavior." Understanding human instincts can expand designers' awareness and available tools, and we can't afford to ignore anything that can stimulate positive feelings, more care, and better work habits all at the same time. Should everything look like babies and puppies? No, but designers can be savvier about making things that appeal to the instinctive desire for pleasure and the need to nurture, things that instill greater attention, fondness, and respect for our surroundings. Design can bring out the caretaker in all of us.

Cute or Smart?

Viewing babies and puppies can improve task-oriented performance, and we respond affectionately to anything with round proportions, large heads, and big "eyes."

Look at your face. Using information from dozens of surveys about what facial features are most attractive—rounder shape, wide-set eyes, greater length between the hairline and the bridge of the nose, and so forth—a team of Israeli scientists invented a software-based algorithm of optimal proportions. Applying this "beautification engine" to photographs, it makes slight adjustments and produces images most likely to be judged as attractive—with an 80 percent success rate. Adobe may be licensing the tool to use in Photoshop. "Beauty is merely a function of mathematical distances or ratios," insists one of the researchers, computer scientist Daniel Cohen-Or, who is working on similar software for color harmony. This suggests applicability way beyond photography.

Sustainable graphic design typically concentrates on print media—for example, recycled paper and nontoxic ink. How might graphics evolve around the ecology of imagery? Could designers adapt "beautification engines" to ensure their work has wider appeal? Could Web and game designers learn from nature's visual rules to create sites and experiences that are easier on the eyes? Consumers use online software to refine their taste in everything from music, books, and movies to dating, and designers use intelligent digital models to optimize geometry, structure, environmental performance, and cost. Why not beauty?

> Beauty is more than skin deep. It's an emotional experience as well as a physical pleasure.

Critics complain that using a formula to create art or design leads to work that is, in Norman's words, "safe and effective, but invariably dull." For example, in 1993, artists Vitaly Komar and Alexander Melamid conducted a worldwide poll to identify people's favorite colors, scenes, and compositions and used this information to produce a series of landscape paintings that are, to say the least, mundane. Yet, averaging preferences is unnatural and overlooks a phenomenon biologists call the "supernormal response," or "peak shift." Often people and other animals prefer embellished or exaggerated versions of the most familiar images, even if those versions never actually occur in nature. Wired to seek the best and brightest of anything, possibly as an adaptation to genetic variation, we look for obvious visual cues of preferred patterns, which could account for makeup and cosmetic surgery, says E. O. Wilson: "The entire beauty industry can be interpreted as the manufacture of supernormal stimuli." Automated processes won't work if they merely seek the least common denominator, but by drawing from subtle natural patterns they could help create images that are more deeply satisfying.

Behind such techniques is scientific research that can help designers understand better why people treasure some things and not others. Beauty is more than skin deep; it is as much an emotional experience as it is a physical pleasure. The mechanics of affection, the mathematics of attraction, can help ensure that images and objects will resonate with people and create lasting social and environmental value. This isn't manipulation—it's sustenance. To sustain interest, design has to keep delivering on its promise to fulfill our desires, and, write Khaslavsky and Shedroff, "the more closely the promise connects with the goals and emotional aspirations of its viewers, the more deeply it begins to seduce." While every viewer is different, we all share emotional instincts that could become standard knowledge for designers.

"When you look at what people find attractive, it is consistent across cultures," evolutionary psychologist Hanne Lie has said. "We have some innate or hardwired beauty detector." Our response is not so much cultural as it is chemical, she explains, since looking at beautiful things fires up the same reward circuitry in the brain that food and narcotics do. As *Science News* put it: "Eye candy might more appropriately be called brain candy." Growing research reveals a universal, biological basis for visual preferences that often transcend individual and cultural differences. Some call it "neuro-aesthetics" and "bio-aesthetics." Psychologically and physiologically, all of us to some degree are drawn consistently to certain shapes, patterns, proportions, and spaces we find deeply satisfying. Brain scientists V. S. Ramachandran and Diane Rogers-Ramachandran outline a "neurology of aesthetics," six "universal laws" that "may cut across not only cultural boundaries but across species boundaries as well. Can it be a coincidence that we find birds and butterflies attractive even though they evolved to appeal to other birds and butterflies, not to us?" To paraphrase Wilson, beauty is in the genes of the beholder.

Wilson was among the first to propose that because for the first 98 percent of our history the human brain evolved in a particular environment, namely the African savanna, we unconsciously have sought—and built— similar spatial cues everywhere since leaving that place some fifty thousand years ago. Across the globe, rolling terrains dotted with stands of trees and modest bodies of water populate parks, gardens, greens, and golf courses. Landscape design is a kind of archaeology of the unconscious that mines the distant memory, locked in our collective minds, of the cradle of our race. Home is where the genome is.

Wilson outlined the savanna theory in *Biophilia* (1984), and a few decades later it is gaining traction among designers. Meaning literally "love of life," biophilia centers on the instinctive bond between people and other living things, and researchers such as Gordon Orians, Roger Ulrich, Judith Heerwagen, Stephen Kellert, and others have shown consistently that abundant access to natural light, views of landscapes, daily and seasonal cycles, and other earmarks of nature have myriad benefits for health and well-being.

Shape for Pleasure.
After Judith Heerwagen.
Three kinds of *biophilia*, attraction to nature's aesthetics. Design can embody the qualities and organizing principles of nature—with all its related benefits—without slavishly copying natural forms.

Literal Biophilia.
Behnisch Architects, Institute for Forestry and Nature Research.
Vegetation-filled atrium.

Facsimile Biophilia.
Darren Petrucci, VH R-10 gHouse.
Leaf-motif ceiling.

Evocative Biophilia.
Cook + Fox, LIVE/WORK/HOME house.
Treelike perforated facade.

The way architects typically embrace this body of research is simply to provide more access to vegetation, indoor or outdoor. Yet, biophilia doesn't necessarily refer to nature's hidden processes, some invisible chemical dependency on other living things. First and foremost it involves our *sensory* experience of nature—we thrive on the visible rhythms and vivid textures of the living world. Wilson makes this clear: "With aesthetics we return to the central issue of biophilia." Heerwagen, an environmental psychologist and author of many of the landmark studies in this field, distinguishes between three kinds of biophilia— *literal* (actual natural material, such as plants and gardens), *facsimile* (photographic reproduction and realistic representation), and *evocative* (nonrepresentational images that emulate nature's order). As Heerwagen's third type suggests, design can embody the qualities and organizing principles of nature—with all their accompanying gifts—without slavishly copying natural forms. This revelation alone could revolutionize aesthetics.

> The revelations of some scientific research could revolutionize design and aesthetics.

Connection: Shape for Place

We often speak of "the environment" in the singular, which suggests one unvarying continuum rather than an endlessly diverse series of unfolding terrains, peaks and plains, hills and haddocks, woodlands and wetlands. For early peoples and indigenous cultures, however, concepts of the universe arise from experience in a particular setting—their worldview depends on an actual view of the world. Space is not a vast void, as conceived by modern minds, for every locality has a particular meaning and is honored as such.

In Homer's *Odyssey*, the hero has carved the frame of his bed from the trunk of a great olive tree rooted under the sleeping chamber; the house is entangled in its environment, inextricable from the living tree. Home is a grounded place. The Greek root of "ecology," *oikos*, means "home," an understanding of place familiar to indigenous peoples. Native American activist Winona LaDuke describes the task of sustainability using the Anishinaabeg word *keewaydahn*—"going home." Ecology is rooted in home, and home is rooted in place. Sustainability is less about energy efficiency than it is about

"A Part of Place."
(a) Anasazi Cliff Dwelling (Mesa Verde); (b)
Icelandic Turf Farm; (c) Igloo.
In many indigenous and vernacular building
traditions, architecture and land unite.

keeping house, both in the sense of design and in the sense of one's family "tree."

In the Kalahari desert, the Gikwe Bushmen, hunter-gatherers known as the First People, lived until recently as all of humanity did during its first 150,000 years. Even in that seemingly barren landscape, writes ethnographer Elizabeth Thomas, the Gikwe "know every bush and stone, every convolution of the ground, and have usually named every place in it where a certain kind of veld food may grow, even if that place is only a few yards in diameter, or where there is only a patch of tall arrow grass or a bee tree, and in this way each group of people knows many hundreds of places by names."

For millennia, the Aboriginal peoples of Australia have passed along their intimate knowledge of place through storytelling whose characters are "song-lines," physical features in the land. The Aranda consider themselves and their entire ancestry inseparable from the terrain—their genealogy and geography are one and the same. "You see this rock?" goes an Aboriginal Dreamtime song. "This rock's me!" For the Western Apache, explains anthropologist Keith Basso, "mountain and arroyos step in symbolically for grandmothers and uncles."

In preclassical civilizations and indigenous peoples, this intimate commingling of people and place may be thought of as *natural culture*. For such a community, its entire culture—its social structure, values, ethos, and aesthetics—evolves out of a specific setting. Being intimately tied to a place, you instinctively give value to everything around you—a tree, a grove, a stream, stone, mound, or meadow all take on sacred significance. But when we lose our bond with the land, things lose their worth. The earliest occurrence of this might have been when the Greeks first ran low on timber, began sailing abroad, conquering other peoples, and taking timber from the occupied lands. Ancient Greece evolved from a particular setting and grew into what is considered the birthplace of all Western civilization, during the Hellenic period, when classical art and philosophy flourished—along with colonialism, the beginning of globalization.

Activist Vandana Shiva explains in *Earth Democracy* that globalization has two meanings: "It can refer to our universal humanity, to cultures of compassion and solidarity, to our common identity as earth citizens. . . . [But] the dominant meaning and form of globalization is economic or corporate globalization . . . in which everything is a commodity, everything is for sale, and the only value a thing has is the price it can bring in the global marketplace." This second form of globalization has a flattening effect, ridding the earth of natural and cultural diversity. "The concrete context of culture—the food we eat, the clothes we wear, the languages we speak, the faiths we hold—is the source of our human identity. However, economic globalization has hijacked culture, reducing it to a consumerist monoculture" of fast food chains.

In *Fast Food Nation*, Eric Schlosser argues that restaurant chains have done to the American landscape what they have done to the American diet—that is, made it homogeneous. The birth of the commercial strip during the postwar era, he recounts, was brought about almost singlehandedly by McDonald's, the first company to apply modern assembly line techniques to restaurants. Standardization has allowed such chains to expand exponentially, and now the top few open a new franchise every couple of hours—fast buildings for fast food. Suburban housing developments imitate fast food tactics, and the "McMansion" has become as ubiquitous as the restaurant that inspired its name. According to surveys, the Golden Arches are the world's most widely recognized symbol, more recognizable than the Christian cross. One of the largest single owners of retail property, with over 32,000 locations in 119 countries, McDonald's has had a significant influence on land use. Its slogan "one taste worldwide" could apply just as well to its buildings, for the inescapable mansard hut looks pretty much the same between Iceland and Egypt, Poland and Portugal, Mexico and Morocco, Serbia and Switzerland, Kuwait and Korea.

> "My relation to this place is part of myself."
>
> —*Arne Naess*

Architects frown on generic development, condemning corporate chains for failing to distinguish one place from another, but at the same time they applaud their own profession for doing the same thing. The most celebrated architects today repeat their own personal styles everywhere they go. Frank Gehry's work may be exciting (and expensive), but its attitude toward place is glorified franchising. When every project is seen as another opportunity to peddle the same wares, economic globalization becomes architectural globalization.

Gehry is routinely criticized for not incorporating basic green practices and especially for having dismissed such practices as "bogus"; yet, even if every Gehry building became carbon neutral, should he or any architect, regardless of talent or popularity, reproduce the same imagery everywhere? Aside from the technological and mechanical impact of construction on climate change, the most damaging effects of design could be the failure to embrace place and enhance local identity. "You can create desolate wastelands of the spirit as well as of the environment," writes architecture critic Ada Louis Huxtable. "You can scar people as well as land."

The lack of difference from place to place devastates culture no less than nature. Many biologists believe that biodiversity is the single most important aspect of ecology, and arguably cultural diversity is equally essential for community. Shiva insists that cultural diversity is the cornerstone of sustainability: "Living cultures evolve from our connectedness with all life. Cultures are based on identity. However, corporate globalization and fundamentalism reduce and manipulate our identities. . . . These diverse, multiple identities shape our sense of self and who we are. And these diversities are not inconsistent with our common humanity. Without diversity, we have no humanity." Ecologist Arne Naess writes that "my relation to this place is part of myself; if this place is destroyed, something in me is destroyed." And, according to philosopher Simone Weil: "To be rooted is perhaps the most important and least recognized need of the human soul." We long to belong.

Design can play a dramatic role in supporting cultural diversity by celebrating the differences between one place and another. The root of the word *culture*, like *cultivation*, means "tilling," developing the land, and customs of building, furniture, cooking, and clothing all traditionally evolve around local ingredients, often the same ones. For South Pacific islanders, the heart of the sago palm provided a staple starch, while its leaves served as strands for garments and thatching for huts. Untold generations of North American Plains Indians hunted the bison for meals, clothing, jewelry, and shelter, so the trappings of an entire culture stemmed from one animal.

Rooted in the Local.
Renzo Piano Building Workshop, Jean-Marie Tjibaou Cultural Center, Nouméa, New Caledonia. The shell-shaped wood-slat towers echo local vernacular building traditions while also coaxing the breeze up from below in this sticky climate.

We think of "home-cooked meals" as especially nourishing, as comfort food. We need home-cooked *homes* too. The image of architecture can enhance the identity of a local community by embracing what is unique about that place. The canonical history of architecture mostly chronicles monumental structures conceived as "a place apart" in the Western sacred space tradition. Even today, museums and mansions alike emulate yesterday's temples and churches as artificial Edens. Instead, designers can expand on the many indigenous and vernacular traditions in which building and land unite to become *a part of place,* embodying the unique geographic essence of locale.

The same can happen with furniture, clothing, and any other artifact of design. The hammock originated one thousand years ago in migratory cultures of Central and South America; woven from the bark of the Hamack tree, it traveled light, floated above the ground to fend off insects, and aired itself in the humidity. The low tilt of the Adirondack chair nestled into the mountainous terrain of upstate New York, mingling among the hemlocks from which it was made, its wide arms speaking of lazy summer days. The Joggling bench's springy plank is the very picture of Charleston's narrow porches and hot, sticky evenings. And both use little material—the original Adirondack chair was made from a dozen pieces cut from a single board, and the Joggling bench *is* a single board.

Contemporary design generally has lost the deep connections between community and climate, between people and place. But *material culture* is just that—the physical manifestation of the interactions between culture and nature.

The Aesthetics of Ecology

At first glance, the three principles of conservation, attraction, and connection might seem at odds. How do "universal laws" of attraction and of conservation relate to the unique particularities of place that drive the idea of connection? Yet, in nature, the immutable demands of physics do not hamper creation—they ignite it. All fish must move through water easily, but those that evolved around coral reefs in the tropics look quite different from those that dwell among icebergs in the arctic. While the planet "has gone cycling on according to the fixed law of gravity," wrote Darwin, "endless forms most beautiful and most wonderful have been, and are being evolved."

The aim is not to mass-produce beauty—quite the opposite. Designers can use the best available intelligence to make things and places that are efficient and elegant, relevant and responsive. Together, the three principles outline an aesthetics of ecology that embraces and embodies the intricate ties between community and context, between conservation and comfort.

Compelling examples of any one of the three principles of conservation, attraction, and connection are uncommon enough, but designs that combine all three are rare. The Tjibaou Cultural Center in New Caledonia is one. The shell-shaped wood-slat towers offer a rich tactile image, like banded reeds, that echoes local vernacular building traditions while also playing an essential role in ventilation, coaxing the breeze upward in this sticky climate. At a smaller scale, Robert Corser's simple NOLA Chair, designed to support post-Katrina rebuilding efforts in New Orleans, similarly blends new technology and traditional form. A plywood adaptation of Art Nouveau imagery—appropriate for a city with a strong French history—its digitally cut pattern ships flat but bends into its final form, held together through its own internal stresses. The surprisingly comfortable seat costs about $40 in material, uses roughly half of a single plywood sheet, and increases shipping efficiency eightfold. Even a simple chair can demonstrate the value of shaping things to enhance environmental, emotional, and communal appeal all at once.

"The standard of beauty is the entire circuit of natural forms—the totality of nature," writes Emerson. "Nothing is quite beautiful alone. . . . A single object is only so far beautiful as it suggests this universal grace." We have lost Emerson's concept of beauty as a quality of association, and today we judge things—buildings, objects, people—in isolation. One dictionary defines beauty as "the quality present in a thing or person that gives intense pleasure or deep satisfaction to the mind, whether arising from sensory manifestations (as shape, color, sound, etc.) [or] a meaningful design or pattern." This understanding of the word limits it just to the idea of attraction—"intense pleasure or deep satisfaction"—without placing it in the context of its environmental and natural development. A richer sense of beauty can create things with profound presence and resonance, powerful physical character deeply connected to people and place.

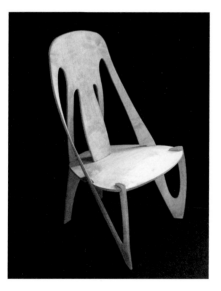

Conserve, Attract, Connect.
Robert Corser, NOLA Chair, New Orleans. Blending new technology and traditional form, it adapts Art Nouveau imagery in a digitally cut pattern that ships flat, with eight times less volume than preformed chairs, uses only half a single plywood sheet, and costs only $40 in material.

Thermal Oasis.
Peter Zumthor, Baths, Vals, Switzerland.
A fully sensory environment of texture,
reverberation, light, mist, and heat.

4 | **Many Senses**

A human being is part of the whole, called by us the universe. . . . He experiences himself, his thoughts and feelings, as something separate from the rest, a kind of optical delusion of his consciousness. This delusion is a kind of prison.

— *Albert Einstein*

EARLY IN THE FINAL DECADE OF THE FIFTEENTH CENTURY, an artist in his Milan workshop took out a notebook, inked his pen, and sketched the figure of a man with four arms and four legs.

Half a millennium later, Leonardo da Vinci's spidery drawing remains one of the most popular images of all time, reproduced and referenced in everything from art to advertising, movies to medicine, fitness to footwear. The "Universal Man," as it's often called, has represented industry on the cover of *BusinessWeek*, Western culture on the Euro coin, and all of humanity on NASA spacesuits. It has been said to symbolize man as the measure of all things, man as the center of all things, man as perfection, and man as divinity—everything to everyone. Venice's Gallerie dell'Accademia, which owns the drawing, calls it "a symbol of classical perfection of body and mind, a microcosm of human scale that is the reflection of cosmos." And in recent years, it has appeared in much of the literature of sustainability to illustrate humanity's union with nature; its meaning, however, couldn't be more different.

The drawing illustrates a passage from Marcus Vitruvius, a Roman architect whose *Ten Books on Architecture*, dating from the first century BC, remains the oldest known treatise on buildings. In it, Vitruvius compares the ideal temple to the human body: "Symmetry is a proper agreement between . . . the different parts and the whole. . . . Thus in the human body there is a kind of symmetrical harmony between forearm, foot, palm, finger, and other small parts; and so it is with perfect buildings." The center point of the human body, he observes, is the navel, from which the outstretched limbs can trace both a circle and a square, the body's height and span being approximately the same, at least in this specimen.

> How our senses interact with the world has everything to do with how we treat the environment.

The idea that the parts should be integral to the whole actually comes from the origin of Western aesthetic theory, Aristotle's *Poetics*, in which he demanded that the plot of a good play and the composition of any good work of art must have a distinct beginning, middle, and end: "For if any part can be inserted or omitted without manifest alteration, it is not a true part of the whole." In other words, the work must be complete in itself—take away any piece, and the whole thing unravels. This opinion has been echoed by artists, designers, and architects from Vitruvius in ancient times to Leonardo, Alberti, and Palladio in the Renaissance and Louis Sullivan, Frank Lloyd Wright, and Le Corbusier in the modern era. Aristotle's idea, the core of both classical and modern aesthetics, has survived intact for over twenty-three centuries.

Critics of the "Universal Man" attack the suggestion that there is an ideal body—namely, the Western white male—that surpasses others. But environmentalists could point out a different problem. Some sources date Leonardo's drawing from 1492, the same year his compatriot and exact contemporary Columbus sailed the ocean blue and stumbled into the New

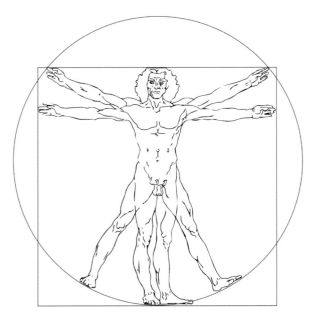

World, but the sketch didn't circulate widely until the early nineteenth century. Produced at the outset of the Age of Exploration and popularized at the dawn of the Industrial Era, the image expresses the sense of entitlement—man as measure—that arguably led to today's environmental crisis. It is the very icon of the attitude that humanity is privileged and the planet belongs to us.

More directly, as a model for aesthetics, the image of the human body as complete in and of itself suggests that design should be the same—closed, autonomous, separate from the world. The "Universal Man" reduces anatomy to geometry and portrays the body—and humanity in general—not as an integral part of nature but, rather, as independent from it. The philosophical basis for both classical and modern aesthetics fundamentally contradicts the idea of ecology.

Chapter 3 outlined three principles—Conservation, Attraction, and Connection—as the basis for an aesthetics of ecology. This chapter and the next explore the links between ecology and the sensory experience. Philosophically, aesthetics concerns the nature of beauty; scientifically, it studies the relationship between the senses and our surroundings. How our bodies interact with the world has everything to do with how we view and treat the environment. Understanding the mechanics of this interaction better is essential to sustainable design.

Two Views of the Human Body.

(a) Leonardo's sketch of the perfect man; (b) thermal image of a crowd. Western aesthetics portrays the human body as self-contained and complete. The aesthetics of ecology must understand the body as an integral part of its surroundings, exchanging energy with the environment.

We Are the World

If we are to rethink aesthetics around the principles of ecology, we must look at our bodies differently. In contrast to the Western classical view, indigenous peoples often view themselves as one with their environments, and they decorate their bodies as such. The mud paint and feather headdresses of Amazonian tribal wear make a wardrobe out of the rain forest. And the leaves and vines that accessorize the Surma and Mursi peoples of Africa's lower Omo valley smudge the lines between person and land. "The body is seen almost as a piece of territory," writes Hans Silvestri about the Omo peoples, "with skin and flesh replacing the stone, ceramics and textiles typical of other cultures." Philosophically and physically, people who live with the land are intimate with the terrain.

The perception that we are separate from our surroundings, says Einstein, is false, "a kind of optical delusion," and science bears this out. In *The Ages of Gaia*, biologist James Lovelock writes: "Living organisms are open systems in the sense that they take and excrete energy and matter. In theory, they are open as far as the bounds of the Universe; but they are also enclosed within a hierarchy of internal boundaries." The human body is a conduit for the flux and flow of energy and matter, a way station for fluids and gases. You are what you eat, but you are also what you breathe, touch, hear, and see. You ingest the sky, eat the earth, and sip the sea. Oceans stream through the brine of your blood and sweat.

> You are what you eat—and what you breathe, touch, hear, and see.

Every time we open our mouths and lungs, we take in trillions of tiny bits of air, water, minerals, and life; they swirl inside us a while before we exhale or excrete them. "A breath," writes Diane Ackerman in *A Natural History of the Senses*, "is not neutral or bland—it's *cooked air*; we live in a constant simmering. There is a furnace in our cells, and when we breathe we pass the world through our bodies." This happens twenty-three thousand times a day. With every breath, we bathe in a bubbling stew of chemistry and biology that doesn't truly belong to us. Of the trillions of cells in the body, only one in ten is human—the other nine are bacteria, viruses, and other microbes swarming in our guts and on our skins. The body is a vast colony of microorganisms, a teeming community of other lives. You are not alone in there.

No man is an island—at 70 percent water, he's more like an archipelago, a sandbar of skin ringing an internal tide pool. You are a messy mass of hot and wet, stuffed into a beautiful bag of bones, and the pores of the skin constantly open and close to let out heat and sweat. But your body doesn't stop at your skin. The difference between your internal temperature and the air around you wraps you in a blanket of warmth—your *aura*, from the Greek word for breath, is the atmosphere to your body's earth. Somewhere inside this thick gradient of heat—up to a meter deep—is, thermally, where you fade into the world.

The body's surface pulsates with energy—a 2,000-calorie daily diet represents about 100 watts, like a living lightbulb. The heat emanating from the entire human race, all 7 billion of us, equals the electrical output of six hundred nuclear power plants. One body generates more bio-electricity than a 120-volt battery and more than 25,000 BTUs of heat. We don't just sing the body electric—we live it. Designers are investigating how to capture body heat to fuel everything from wristwatches and cell phones to whole buildings.

We are walking flame, human ovens, and everything we eat, make, or wear feeds this fire. Naturalist William Bryant Logan ruminates on the burning bush of Exodus: "Moses does not see a technicolor fantasy. He sees the bush as it really is. . . . Plants (and animals) unlock their stored sunlight and turn it into heat energy that fuels their motion, their feeling, their thought, or whatever their living consists of. All that is living burns. This is the fundamental fact of nature."

The fundamental fact of humanity is not just that we are *in* nature—it's that we *are* nature. We are the world, quite literally, products of our natural and artificial environment both. So when we talk about the ecology of design, we're not just talking about shaving a few kilowatts off our energy bills. Design can embrace humanity's place in nature by fortifying the bonds between body and world. The things we make, from our clothing to our communities, are the medium through which and in which we interpret, experience, and live our worlds. They can construct barriers or conduits, blocking or building pathways between us and everything else.

Design can bedevil us with disease and destruction—from toxic materials in toys to crime-provoking urbanism—or it can revel in the glories of being alive. "Life showers over everything, radiant, gushing," Ackerman announces. "We need to return to feeling the textures of life. Much of our experience . . . is an effort to get away from those textures, to fade into a stark, simple, solemn, puritanical, all-business routine that doesn't have anything so unseemly as sensuous zest." Much of the experience of design, even much of routine sustainable design, is also stark, solemn, puritanical, and all business. We yearn for that unseemly, sensuous zest, and design can help quench our craving.

"We may think of the sensing body as a kind of open circuit that completes itself only in things, and in the world," writes David Abram in *The Spell of the Sensuous*. Rich, fully sensory experiences make us feel more alive. We gather them with gusto, grab the world and yank it closer. Our appreciation for things wells up, because when we feel better, we care better. Pleasure builds value, and joy brings reverence, so design for the senses can fulfill both our moral and animal instincts.

The modern mind believes that intellect is all that matters. Descartes supposedly thought of his mantra "I think, therefore I am" while in a state of sensory deprivation, holed up in a box or an old oven. Yet, as Ackerman points out, when we call ourselves "sentient" beings, we invoke the original meaning, *sentire,* "to feel." We are sensory beings—I *feel,* therefore I am. "There is no way in which to understand the world without first detecting it through the radar-net of our senses," Ackerman insists. Our tools can expand our senses, but they are never more—and never less—than blips on that radar. Design must *make sense*, in every sense of the phrase.

> We are sensory beings—I feel, therefore I am.

"The Hidden Sense"

Design can appeal to the whole body, for we feel with our entire being. "Most people think of the mind as being located in the head," says Ackerman, "but the latest findings in physiology suggest that *the mind* doesn't really dwell in the brain but travels the whole body on caravans of hormone and enzyme, busily making sense of the compound wonders we catalogue as touch, taste, smell, hearing, vision." Nerves sweep across the skin in swaths called dermatomes, linking remote territories of the body like anatomical trade winds or physiological gulf streams.

Our senses interconnect, blending in the mixers of our minds. We tell ourselves we see or hear things separately from touching or tasting them, but our instincts throw them together—*synesthesia* it's called. The phenomenon stems from an older, more primitive part of the brain than the cortex, where cognitive functions reside. Some people experience it profoundly, unavoidably smelling sound or hearing texture. Many inescapably associate certain colors with particular letters or numbers, seeing the word *plane* as mint green or the number *4* as dark brown. Until recently, the "hidden sense" was considered abnormal or even pathological, but in truth we all experience it to some degree.

Babies are synesthetes. According to developmental psychologists Daphne and Charles Maurer, a newborn doesn't perceive smell as coming through the nose alone: "He hears odors, and sees odors, and feels them too. His world is a melee of pungent aromas—and pungent sounds, and bitter-smelling sounds, and sweet-smelling sights, and sour-smelling pressures against the skin. If we could visit the newborn's world, we would think ourselves inside a hallucinogenic perfumery." Imagine design that dwells in all the senses together, simultaneously, triggering pleasures across the bounds we've learned to divide one from another. Synesthesia is ecology felt in our bodies.

In taste tests for the soft drink 7-Up, whether people detect more lime or lemon can depend on whether the label has more green or yellow, respectively. Marketing researcher Louis Cheskin dubs this "sensation transference," when people unconsciously translate the character of the packaging into the experience of the product. A sprig of parsley on the label, says Cheskin, can make canned meat taste fresher. We prefer peaches in glass jars, not metal cans, and ice cream in round containers, not square boxes. Margarine must be yellow. The more intense the color of a fruit beverage, the sweeter the taste.

Clinical synesthesia may be an extreme condition, but its lessons can help designers cultivate a multisensory approach to design. Oxford psychologist Charles Spence champions a new philosophy based on full-body stimulation: "Sensism has the potential to deliver a society-wide antidote to the stresses of modern living in the form of a multi-sensory boost. It requires the creation of new sensory environments that consider everything from the color of walls and the ambient scent of our surrounds to the background music playing and the texture of our food, flooring and furnishings."

Sensory pleasures appeal to the animal in us—that's why we call them "creature comforts"—and our instincts are closer to nature than our intellects are. Would that we could tune ourselves to our environments with the sensitivity of whales, who navigate the vast depths by sensing the planet's magnetic fields. Many fish detect the slightest quivering of water from miles away, and elephants feel the faintest movement of earth, which enabled them to head for higher ground before the Indian Ocean tsunami hit in 2004. The human body is designed to connect more completely with the sensual world, but generally we've lost that ability because culture teaches us to focus on mind over matter. Design can tease out our natural affinity for the living earth.

"We still perceive the world," writes Ackerman, "in all its gushing beauty and terror, right on our pulses. There is no other way. To begin to understand

Utility Garden.
Cero9, Power Station, Ames, Iowa.
The architects propose to cover the
existing power plant with a monumental
trellis of native roses (and micro
wind turbines), which would fill the air
with fragrance, make a huge habitat
for birds and bees, and turn a
monstrosity into a feast
for the eyes—and nose.

the gorgeous fever that is consciousness, we must try to understand the senses . . . and what they can teach us about the ravishing world we have the privilege to inhabit." More and more, new research reveals how everyday sights, sounds, smells, tastes, and textures influence the unconscious mind. Aesthetic delight is a powerful motivator, firing up the pleasure centers of the brain, the "hedonic hot spots," as neurobiologists call them. In brain scan studies at Caltech, the sight of a well-designed product such as an iPod, an Aeron chair, or a Capresso coffeepot triggered an involuntary surge of those synapses in the motor cerebellum that govern hand movement. Instinctively, we reach out for attractive things. Beauty literally moves us.

Scents and Sensibility

Aesthetic pleasure isn't purely visual, and scent is a potent stimulus. The poet Schiller sniffed rotting apples to overcome writer's block, and Yale researchers have found that the smell of spiced apples has an exhilarating effect that can fend off panic attacks. According to a Dutch study, people tidy up more when there's a hint of citrus in the air. By contrast, people who lose their sense of smell can become depressed more easily than people who lose their vision. Although the human olfactory mechanism isn't nearly as strong as that of many other species, it is keen nevertheless. To activate the impulse of smell in a nerve ending requires only eight molecules of a substance, and we can distinguish between ten thousand different odors.

"Nothing," claims Ackerman, "is more memorable than a smell." Cleopatra scented the sails of her ship so that the wind carried news of her impending arrival up the Nile. Ancient potentates built whole palaces of cedarwood for its sweet smell of resin and its natural ability to ward off insects. In *The Eyes of the Skin: Architecture and the Senses,* Juhani Pallasmaa contends that aroma can be the most identifiable trait of a space or place. "I cannot remember the appearance of the door to my grandfather's farmhouse in my early childhood," he recounts, "but I do remember the resistance of its weight and the patina of its wood surface scarred by decades of use, and I recall especially vividly the scent of home that hit my face as an invisible wall behind the door. Every dwelling has its individual smell of home."

Entire cities can be defined by their fragrances. Streetscapes fill with the aroma of roasting coffee spilling from Seattle cafés, or the bouquet of fruit and flowers at Amsterdam markets, or the sugar and cinnamon wafting out of Viennese pastry shops. The northern Spanish town of San Sebastián, set in a deep cover ringed by cliffs, remains one of the most spectacular places I know, but its most unforgettable feature has to be the distinctive scent of sea and sand lingering in the air of the old fishing village at its heart.

We associate so many places with their aromatic landscapes—the eucalyptus groves of Northern California, for example—and the olfactory pleasures of gardens laced with basil, thyme, mint, lilac, and lavender can be extraordinarily beneficial for physical health and emotional well-being. Aromatherapy can relieve stress, headaches, muscles, and inflammation and improve sleep, digestion, blood circulation, and the immune system. The most primal of our senses, smell also is the only one with a direct link to the brain, passing straight from the environment through the nose to the limbic system, triggering the release of endorphins.

The medicinal properties of scent have been cultivated since antiquity and were a particular fascination of medieval monks in their cloistered gardens. Today, fragrant herbs and flowers are common in healing gardens—for example, jasmine bushes planted outside the windows of San Francisco's Laguna Honda Hospice. Aroma gardens for the blind are becoming more popular, as well. Helen Keller felt it wasn't she but the sighted who are blind, "for they have no idea how fair the flower is to the touch, nor do they appreciate its fragrance, which is the soul of the flower."

Skin Deep

Sometimes called "the mother of the senses," touch is the most immediate way to experience the world. One medical researcher describes it as the basis for all the other senses: "The tongue and palate sense the food; the ear, sound waves; the nose, emanations; the eyes, rays of light." While we can see, hear, and smell from a distance, touch is up close and personal, our most social sense. Unlike vision, hearing, taste, and smell, which concentrate on single organs, the sensation of touch is distributed over the entire body. Skin, the largest organ, averages twenty-two square feet in surface area, the size of a walk-in closet. We are entirely tactile beings.

Because we can't "turn it off" the way we close our eyes or plug our ears, touch remains constantly present. It's the first sense to develop, for embryos begin to respond to tactile stimulation even before they develop eyes or ears, and newborns grab with their hands before opening their eyes the first time.

As we age, we continue to feel long after eyesight and hearing fade, so touch is both our first and last sense. We are most sensitive at our lips, the soles of our feet, the palms of our hand, and our fingers. Touch receptors, nerve endings devoted to tactile stimulation, are most plentiful in these areas, and about a hundred of them reside in each of your fingertips.

Touch defines us. We crave it—we *need* it. Regular touch eases stress and anxiety, improves breathing and heart rate, hastens healing, and increases mental aptitude and productivity. The calming effect can be immediate, and just lightly caressing someone's hand can lower blood pressure. Babies' physical, mental, and emotional development progresses better when they are routinely massaged, yet, compared to other cultures, Americans are touch starved. One study discovered that American preschoolers are touched less than 12 percent of the time, and without regular contact people of all ages get sicker more often. Japan and France are much more touchy-feely, which may be one reason their life expectancies are greater; worldwide, they respectively rank first and tenth for longevity. The United States is thirty-eighth.

"Touch seems to be as essential as sunlight."

—*Diane Ackerman*

"Touch seems to be as essential as sunlight," notes Ackerman, but designers have yet to learn it. While research into the benefits of sunlight has become the backbone of conventional green design, little attention has been paid to touch. Tactile stimulation should be a vital ingredient in design, since touch need not come from other people, or even from living things. Hospitals have found that placing newborns on natural lambskin blankets can improve the infants' health, weight, body heat, sleep, and mood. The tradition of "swaddling" has been shown to alleviate stress, and a snug-fitting blanket can relax an infant enough to lower its heart rate. The quieting effect of keeping babies outdoors may be due, in part, to the movement of the air across the skin, so natural ventilation, normally recommended to save electricity and freshen the air, could also bring tactile and emotional comfort through its gentle caress.

In many cultures, designed objects such as "worry" beads or polished stones have been used for centuries to stimulate the hands and promote general relaxation and meditation. Studies of brain wave patterns confirm the calming effects of Catholic rosary beads and Chinese Baoding balls, and manufactured products such as stress sponges are marketed to offer similar benefits. Often such products are used to alleviate the adverse effects of overusing other products, such as a computer keyboard or mouse. Why not combine the two by giving the original products the stress-reducing traits of

Please Touch.

Michael Roopenian, Engrain Keyboard.
The rippled wood grain gives every key a
different texture, aiding typing, accuracy
(through haptic memory), and pleasure.
According to the designer, it "uses nature's
tactility to strengthen the relationship
between user and interface."

the others—a squeezable mouse, for example, or a dimpled keyboard. Could
typing on a computer please and strengthen the hands instead of causing
repetitive stress injuries?

Spatial environments can be enlivened by the visual promise of tactile pleasure. At the Finnish Embassy in Washington, DC, the walls of the
elevator banks are clad in unfinished copper, and the oils from your skin
leave a patina in the shape of a handprint, evidence of intimate habita-
tion. The dipped edge of a marble tread in an old library wears down with
many years of footfalls—"time turned into shape," writes Pallasmaa. "It is
pleasurable to press a door handle shining from the thousands of hands
that have entered the door before us; the clean shimmer of ageless wear has
turned into an image of welcome and hospitality. The door handle is the
handshake of the building."

Traditional Japanese houses are highly textured environments—barefoot
soles enjoy woven matting on the floors, and grainy wood and paper parti-
tions appeal to the hands and eyes. Mosque floors are covered in rich carpets
that stimulate the nerves in the feet and knees. Wood wainscoting protects
walls but also offers warmth to the touch. Finnish architect Alvar Aalto
wrapped columns in rope or rattan where the body might brush against or

grab hold. Tactile posts are especially effective, since touch receptors are more sensitive in the vertical direction.

Cobblestone streets fill entire cities with vivid texture. The walks and walls along the historic riverfront of Savannah, Georgia, are populated by ballast stones ejected from sailing ships to make room for cargo. When set in sand, cobbles have the environmental advantage of being permeable to rainwater and more durable than homogeneous paving, which cracks. Some of Rome's *sampietrini* ("little stones of St. Peter's") have lasted two thousand years—Eternal City indeed. Originally, these stones were intended in part to give horse hoofs better traction, but recent research shows that they're good for human feet as well. Geriatric studies at the Oregon Research Institute discovered that regularly walking barefoot on cobbles, outdoors or in, improves blood pressure, balance, and strength. In the Urban Aeration concept, Konyk Architecture envisions whole cities composed of porous materials that absorb carbon and clean the air, but the richly tactile design could benefit the skin as well as the sky.

Porous City.
Konyk Architecture, Urban Aeration.
The designers envision whole cities composed of porous materials that absorb carbon and clean the air, but the richly tactile design could benefit the skin as well as the sky.

A Warm Body

When we touch or even look at materials, we often associate their texture with climate. At Ranchos de Taos, New Mexico, where the temperature can swing from blazing hot to bone-chilling cold in a single day, the unbelievably smooth adobe on the four-foot-thick walls of the San Francisco des Asis Church promises the delivery of warmth into the palms of your hands. By contrast, woven reed-and-thatch huts in the sticky climes of Thailand, Africa, or the Ukraine signal a light and airy shelter of breathing walls. The relative temperatures of materials invite or discourage interaction with our surroundings. Stone is slow to lose its temperature, and metal quick, so we consider the two "warm" and "cold," which is why there aren't many chrome mountain lodges.

The act of touching things that are warmer or colder than we are can dramatically alter our comfort and mood. In *Thermal Delight in Architecture* (1979)—still one of the few eloquent reveries on the cultural and aesthetic significance of environmental design—Lisa Heschong celebrates the "simple pleasure" of holding a cool stone or a warm cup of coffee. "There is something very affirming of one's own life in being aware of these little pieces of information about the world outside us," she writes. "When the sun is warm on my face and the breeze is cool, I know it is good to be alive."

We transfer this experience to our belongings, whose warmness can inspire great sympathy. "Like the toddler," writes Heschong, "we tend to cherish the things that have provided us with warmth or coolness just when we needed or wanted it. This association between an object and our thermal well-being may become semiconscious and vague, and yet it can strongly contribute to our affection for the object. How hard it is to give up the old misshapen sweater or the old shade hat that kept the sun off for so long. They are rather like old friends who have done us a good turn over and over again."

Recent findings suggest that the pleasure of warmth can even cause us to like people more. In a study at Yale, lab assistants carrying armloads of books, papers, and clipboards bumped into students in the hall and asked them to hold a cup of coffee. If the coffee was iced, the students tended to judge the person as cold and antisocial; if hot, they considered the person warm and affable.

The social dimension of thermal pleasure can be profound, and until relatively recently it had a dramatic influence on community rituals and habits. Public places offer the refreshment of open and temperate space; the expansive stone surfaces of an Italian *piazza* radiate warmth in the chilly evenings and coolness during hot days. The Mediterranean custom of the evening promenade, or *paseo,* developed to take advantage of cooler streets in the evening. Barcelona's *La Rambla*, one of the most inviting thoroughfares anywhere, is both the social and thermal heart of the city.

In traditional homes, the location of rooms chased the light and warmth: breakfast was in the east, reading along the south, the parlor at the west, and so forth. Families moved outdoors when hot and indoors when cold. The concept of a *sustainable floor plan* isn't part of the green building vocabulary, but it's essential to both conservation and comfort. In German architect Thomas Herzog's house in Waldmohr, the warmest spaces, such as bathrooms, occupy the center, with the temperature decreasing gradually toward the perimeter— a "thermal onion." Conservation and comfort come from protecting the core first, like the human body, or like a tree losing its leaves in winter.

The sacred spaces of many cultures traditionally are defined by their thermal character. In Saudi Arabian mosques, the subterranean prayer hall stays cool on even the hottest days. The English hearth, the Finnish sauna, the Korean *k'ang,* Roman *thermae,* Turkish baths, and Native American sweat lodges provide warmth but also play socially and culturally significant roles in their societies. "In the sauna," goes an old Finnish expression, "one must conduct oneself as one would in a church." Saunas and baths can lower tension, loosen muscles, aid circulation, clear the lungs, strengthen the immune system, and improve the complexion. Benjamin Franklin, who brought the first bathtub to the United States in the 1780s, routinely wrote while enjoying a soak. "There must be quite a few things a hot bath won't cure," mused Sylvia Plath, "but I don't know many of them."

The modern "amenity" of air-conditioning virtually extinguished our cultural rituals and habits; when any space anywhere can be tempered artificially, climate has little bearing on how we shape our homes, communities, and lives. In the name of comfort, we've cut ourselves off from the world, and the intimate association between "hearth and home"—redundant words in some languages—has disappeared along with the hearth itself. (Now we consider the "working fireplace" a luxury.) The mechanisms of artificial heating and cooling typically bring no social, cultural, or aesthetic richness to a place. Unsightly, noisy necessities, they're hidden away in the attic or basement.

Shaping our spaces and places more intelligently so we don't have to rely completely on these machines can save enormous amounts of energy. In 2006, the United States used about 4 quadrillion BTUs for air-conditioning alone—more than the total energy usage of most other countries. Of course, we can cut this consumption significantly by designing buildings to channel heat and air naturally, without electrical assistance. But smarter design can also bring back sacredness and delight by rousing the body and bringing in the outside world. In tempering our artificial environments, architects and engineers default toward uniformity, but the body was designed to experience changing temperatures, and we long for variety. Many cultural rituals around baths and saunas hinge on contrast, and Scandinavians often jump naked into a snowbank or ice pool before the sauna. "Truly to enjoy bodily warmth," writes Herman Melville, "some small part of you must be cold, for there is no quality in this world that is not what it is merely by contrast."

The Sound of Sustainability

"Every building has a certain temperature," writes Swiss architect Peter Zumthor, whose thermal baths in Vals, Switzerland, are a masterpiece of sensuality. By "temperature," Zumthor means both physical and psychological; buildings are artifacts but also states of beings with moods and temperaments. He uses the word *temper*, as in to "prepare," to suggest tuning a building like a musical instrument. His Swiss Sound Box, a pavilion at the 2000 Hannover Expo, plays with both thermal and acoustic temperature. The structure is an enormous cabinet of larch and pine, warm to both the hand and the ear. Laid up without glue, bolts, or nails, the wood expands and contracts freely. The structure breathes and sings with beautiful timber lungs.

Forty years ago, in *The Architecture of the Well-Tempered Environment*, Reyner Banham almost single-handedly resurrected thermal intelligence in design by subjecting modernism to a scathing environmental critique. Yet, as suggested by the title, an homage to Bach's keyboard opus "The Well-Tempered Clavier," sound is equally essential to the well-tempered environment. More than a play on words, the connection reveals a historical truth. Acoustician Hope Bagenal recounts that early Christian music and liturgy evolved to suit the sound of a single space: the first St. Peter's Basilica, the precursor to the current structure in Rome.

Gregorian chants, as well as the slow, rhythmic oratory of priests' sermons, adapted to the long reverberation time of St. Peter's cavernous interior. The cadence of the Latin language was perfectly compatible with the space, and priests and chanters learned to dwell on a particular pitch, around A or A flat, the building's "sympathetic note," its acoustical sweet spot. The singers found that multipart harmonies were especially powerful, and what grew out of this co-evolution, Bagenal claims, was no less than the entire tradition of Western music: "Polyphonic music, as heard today in Westminster Cathedral [and in every church or concert hall], was directly produced by a building form and by the open vowels of the Latin language."

After the Reformation, church design had to facilitate sermons in local languages instead of Latin, so large expanses of absorptive wood were added to the naked stone, cutting the reverberation time by a third or more. The subtler Lutheran acoustics allowed Bach, the organist at St. Thomas Church in Leipzig, to compose in many different keys and develop the swirling complexities of his audacious fugues. Adding a bit of wood to a building completely changed music history.

But the unique "temperature" of a structure influences all of us, not just musical geniuses, for we all can detect the shape and scale of a space with our ears—a cavernous hall echoes visceral and vast, while a cushioned inglenook wraps us in a soft blanket of sound. A tunnel reverberates with Doppler effects, a dome shudders at the center, and our bodies resonate with these spaces. In folk dance traditions such as the Andalusian flamenco, the Russian *troika,* or an Appalachian hoedown, the room bounces and jumps, and we feel the music in the floorboards and in our bones.

> "Sight is the sense of the solitary observer, whereas hearing creates a sense of connection and solidarity."
>
> —*Juhani Pallasmaa*

The songs of the Kaluli people of Papua New Guinea echo birds, insects, tree frogs, waterfalls, and rain. "Kaluli music is naturally part of the surrounding soundscape," writes ethnomusicologist Steven Feld. "In this rainforest musical ecology, the world really is a tuning fork." Similarly, the density of the rain forest leads the BaMbuti Pygmies of the Congo to rely more on sound than sight, since approaching prey can be detected more easily with the ears than with the eyes. "Sight is the sense of the solitary observer," insists Pallasmaa, "whereas hearing creates a sense of connection and solidarity; our look wanders lonesomely in the dark depths of a cathedral, but the sound of the organ makes us immediately experience our affinity with the space."

Places come alive with their singular sounds. Once I lived in a Greenwich Village studio I will associate forever with the clinking plates and muffled voices of the café across the street. My apartment in Washington, DC, overlooked the exotic bird sanctuary of the National Zoo, and I woke every morning to the barking of flamingos, my own aviary alarm clock. Sound dramatically shapes

The Sound of Silence.

Fuseproject, Mission One Motorcycle.
The fastest electric motor bike available
is marketed for its quietness, advertised
as "the closest thing to flying with
two wheels on the ground."

what filmmakers call *mise-en-scène,* the mood of a setting. Coastal villages breathe with the thrum of the surf, plains towns wail with the sweeping wind, and cities of the north muffle themselves in the snow. The hum of a city is created by the pattern of streets, heights of buildings, prevalent materials, and even architectural styles. The rusticated *palazzi* of Florence strike noise back into the street, the complex curves of Baroque Rome bounce it around, and the arcades of neoclassical Paris contain it at the sidewalk. Cities are urban soundscapes.

Although what we hear is vital to perception, experience, and comfort, it isn't considered vital to sustainable design, and the most popular guidelines exclude acoustics. Conventional green building standards address air pollution and light pollution but not noise pollution, which can be just as harmful to both human and animal populations. Noise can cause anxiety, irritability, hostility, headaches, fatigue, high blood pressure, heart problems, respiratory ailments, and even mental illness. (Etymologically, *noise* relates to *nausea.*) By far the number one impediment to workplace and classroom productivity, noise should be a top priority in the creation of responsive environments. Designers can bone up on acoustic ecology, a growing discipline studying how living things relate to their environments through sound.

Sometimes, it's the absence of sound that brings grace. In buildings, radiant floor heating systems replace whining air ducts with glorious quiet. In cities, electric buses are a welcome respite from traffic's onslaught to the ears. The nonprofit Right to Quiet Society declares: "We want our homes to be havens from unwanted noise, and we ask that the soundscape of our public spaces, like the air we breathe, be respected." Silence is golden.

The Mission One motorcycle, the fastest electric motor bike available, is marketed for its quietness: "What is the sound of speed? Silence. With a top speed of 150mph, the Mission One is the closest thing to flying with two wheels on the ground." Can such a machine hope to compete in the "hear me roar" culture of hogs and Harleys?

But designing for the ears shouldn't just reduce or abolish noise—it should aim to create mellifluous music and sonorous spaces. There's magic in sound. Before the Bronze Age, humanity had never heard resonant sounds other than human voices and animal cries, so the singing emitted from struck metal seemed miraculous. Sacred traditions in many cultures include this music from metal—Catholic *carillions*, Celtic bells, Buddhist chimes, Chinese gongs—and a *campanile*'s call to worship, or a clock tower's signal of the hour, is the most identifiable event in many towns.

In many landscape traditions, artificial sounds stem from the natural environment and climate. Thai rain drums fill gardens with impromptu music during a rain shower. Buried next to the wash basin in a Japanese garden you might find a melodic device called a *suikinkutsu*, an upside-down bowl that snickers with the splash of spilled water. The fountains of Italian gardens spatter with melody while cooling the air. A Slovenian vineyard might be guarded by a *klopotec*, a kinetic scarecrow whose wooden limbs dance and drum in the wind. Gravel in the groundscape of Japanese temples varies in size and changes pitch with your footfalls, slowing your approach and making you tangibly aware of your body and your surroundings.

In *This Is Your Brain on Music,* neuroscientist Daniel J. Levitin shows that music is inherent to every culture because it provides an evolutionary advantage by aiding memory, social cohesiveness, and even sexual selection, and lyrical sound elevates dopamine levels, creating a natural high. Could the environmental "music" of design, properly tuned, satisfy the brain's desires? After all, the formal structure and classical harmonies of what we call music today is a rather recent invention, but our species has enjoyed melodic sound for millennia. The composer John Cage once burst from a soundproof room to declare that there's no such thing as silence. In the absence of other ambient noise, we still hear the gurgling and beating of our own bodies and the vibration of the space around us. For Cage, this is music. For designers, it could be too.

Roof like a Forest.
Ateliers Jean Nouvel, Louvre, Abu Dhabi.
An enormous mesh umbrella lets
dappled sunlight pass through in variegated
patterns, like a forest canopy

5 | Ecology and Imagery

My eyes were made to erase all that is ugly.

—*Raoul Dufy*

LIFE ON EARTH BEGAN 3.8 BILLION YEARS AGO, and for the vast majority of that time, evolution trudged along very, very slowly. Then something happened. Approximately 550 million years ago—about 8:30 at night if the history of life were one day—came a sudden flourishing of biodiversity. Over the course of a million years—a drop in the evolutionary bucket—the number of animal classifications grew by an order of magnitude, mushrooming from three to thirty-eight, the number that remains today. This was the Cambrian explosion, evolution's Big Bang.

What brought about this dramatic burst of new life? Scientists debated this question for a century and a half, until a young zoologist named Andrew

Shaped by Light.
Renzo Piano Building Workshop, Nasher Sculpture Pavilion, Dallas, Texas. The sculpted cast-aluminum sunscreen above the glass roof blocks direct sunlight but allows ambient light and views of the sky.

Parker solved the riddle only a decade ago. Before the Cambrian, the planet was covered in thick dust, gas, and vapor, an atmospheric stew lingering from the birth of the earth. Then the fog began to lift, and the planet's surface got brighter. Newly exposed, creatures that developed sensitivity to light had a huge advantage over their blinded prey, and the race for vision was on. The Cambrian explosion was the origin of sight. The earth had languished in the dark for eons, then brightness lit the fuse of biodiversity and began shaping life as we now know it. Parker calls it the Light Switch Theory.

> We live in a world of light and sight, and we judge things by how they look.

Today, over 95 percent of all animals have eyes. As important as the other senses are, most of what we perceive is what we see, for 70 percent of the human body's sense receptors cluster in the eyes. Vision dominates. We live in a world of light and sight, and we judge things by how they look. In the first tenth of a second after we lay eyes on someone, we judge their trustworthiness, competence, aggressiveness, and likability, and these first impressions often determine how we feel about them months later.

Sustainable design seeks stronger connections to nature, and the eye is a key connector. In fact, research into the benefits of daylight has been the foundation of green building standards and practices, and reams of scientific studies over the past couple of decades have shown that abundant natural light can improve everything from children's performance in schools to employees' productivity in the workplace to patients' recovery in hospitals. According to Roger Ulrich, a pioneer of research in sustainable health care design, patients exposed to morning sunshine need pain medication nearly a quarter less often.

Regular contact with ultraviolet radiation supplies us with vitamin D and spurs melatonin production while also improving sleep, work performance, memory, mood, and even logical reasoning. We also need the natural variation of light over daily and seasonal cycles, without which we get listless and depressed. So it's ironic that many educational facilities in the past—including my own high school, a school for the visual arts—had no windows. But the importance of daylight, now firmly established, is completely changing the design of virtually every building type and even whole cities. In 2010, San Francisco formed a task group to determine the optimal ratio of sunlight to shade in its public spaces.

Nevertheless, in recent years, the standard approach to designing for natural light has stunted corporate architecture. Many green buildings look

Light and Time.
Parabola Architecture, Timepiece House,
Charlottesville, Virginia.
Aligned precisely with solar north,
the house makes the movement of the earth
constantly visible from the interior.
Through an oculus in the roof, a
concentrated beam of daylight pushes
a disc of light across the concrete floor. Light
shapes the space: the living room ceiling
is a conical section traced by the arc of the
sun on the winter solstice, and the central
stairwell follows the noon angle
on the summer solstice.

alike, regardless of location and function, in large part because they share a similar goal with daylight—to flatten it. The most common environmental design standards initially developed for commercial office structures, a building type defined by relatively little variation. The open plan and flexible workspace common in modern offices are considered best served by consistent light levels throughout, so buildings are designed to diffuse daylight uniformly, resulting in repetitive exterior facades and often lackluster interior spaces. The typical green building lacks the rich mystery of the most inspired architecture because it is intentionally monotonous—not too bright, not too dark.

Although our eyes are built to enjoy a certain range in the intensity of light, context can heavily influence the most desirable kind and quantity. The exquisite tracery of the traditional Arabic *Mashrabiya*, a latticed bay window, makes for a dappled scrim of shade, so treasured in the blazing desert. In a very different climate, the Inuit igloo creates an icy shell of soft, milky light. As heat from the body slightly melts the interior surface, the cracks in the joints fill to ensure a perfectly insulated seal with a slick sheen that, when the light emanates through the translucent surface, makes an utterly breathtaking space. A potential liability—our own body heat—beautifully completes the design.

In his lyrical homage to traditional Japanese aesthetics, *In Praise of Shadows*, Jun'ichirō Tanizaki notes that whereas Westerners prefer the soaring, light-filled space of the Gothic cathedral, in the Japanese temple and house "what first strikes the eye is the massive roof of tile or thatch and the heavy darkness that hangs beneath the eaves. Even at midday cavernous darkness spreads over all beneath the roof's edge, making entryway, doors, walls, and pillars all but invisible. . . . In making for ourselves a place to live, we first spread a parasol to throw a shadow on the earth, and in the pale light of the shadow we put together a house." Low, deep overhangs developed over time to keep driving wind and rain off the paper screens that, in lieu of walls, allow the structure to breathe in a wet, humid climate. Living this way, Tanizaki believes, led his ancestors to learn to love the mysteries dwelling in the dark:

"The beauty of a Japanese room depends on a variation of shadows, heavy shadows against light shadows—it has nothing else."

Living Color

Although the importance of intelligent lighting cannot be overstated, its emphasis among green building professionals has distracted from other, equally important aspects of vision, and a great deal of evidence indicates that color, shape, and pattern could have just as much bearing on health and well-being. Depending on application and intensity, color can influence emotion. Complicated by other environmental conditions and rarely experienced in isolation, a particular color may not guarantee a particular reaction, but many studies suggest that we are wired to react to color.

For example, much literature supports the general impression that warm hues stimulate and cool colors calm. In *Color and Human Response,* Faber Birren notes that red can raise blood pressure, pulse rate, tension, respiration, and perspiration, while blue, associated with sky and water, has the reverse effect. One report showed that typing in a red room can lead to more mistakes, and a late-1970s study determining that rosy shades are soothing led to a spate of hospitals and jails painted in "drunk tank pink." More recently, researchers at Texas A&M studied the effects of color on scenic beauty in forest landscapes and found that people invariably were drawn to a certain green-yellow range of the spectrum, while blues and browns detracted from the perception of beauty. And in 2012, German researchers found that just glancing at natural shades of green can boost creativity and motivation. We associate verdant colors with food-bearing vegetation—shades that promise nourishment.

Context and culture can influence how we view color, so our preconceptions might play as big a role as direct perception. Western brides wear white for its purity, but for the Chinese it symbolizes mourning. Nevertheless, the human eye can distinguish more than 10 million different colors, so it stands to reason that color perception serves an essential biological purpose. Advertisements in color are read up to 42 percent more often than the same ads in black and white, and researchers find that color aids memory by helping the brain process and store images more efficiently—a fact that has been used by designers to assist way finding in hospitals, airports, parking garages, and other potentially confusing facilities.

"It is time to reconsider the basic visual elements of three-dimensional design," declares interior designer Shashi Caan, who explains that architects and interior designers tend to begin with a distinctive form, to which color, texture, and pattern are applied after the fact, if at all. "Contemporary design education, which emphasizes form over more intimate visual details, is responsible for the present generation of designers who create tonal gray environments devoid of sufficient visual interest to enliven the human spirit, resulting in a discomforting sensory deprivation." The design process should be reversed, she insists—start with color and light and shape places around nuances of tone and mood. "This will bring a rejuvenation and new hope to our built environments."

Caan complains that designers lack visual literacy and rarely are trained in the science of vision. Color theory generally isn't taught in architecture schools, although it can be a powerful design tool. Warm, bright, saturated colors can appear to advance, while cooler, duller hues recede, so facile designers can use contrast to aid the perception of space, depth, and scale. Knowing that solar orientation affects color rendition—for example, north-facing rooms have a bluish tint because outside light is reflected from the sky—designers can plan a palette that both aids perception and adjusts occupants to the environment outside. According to Caan, color also can influence both physical and social activity. In an experiment with three cocktail lounges that were spatially identical but different in color (one blue, one red, one yellow), her team found that people gestured, fidgeted, and circulated more in the yellow and red rooms but tended to stay still in the blue. They also interacted differently, lining the perimeter in the blue room and clustering toward the middle in the others. Do brighter, warmer shades promote social activity?

According to other studies, color can affect thermal comfort, for people's perception of temperature can change with the color of a space—blue-green can lower the comfort range, and red-orange can raise it. Could this effect reliably reduce dependence on mechanical air-conditioning and save electricity? Maybe, but color can aid conservation more directly. Darker paint absorbs more light, requiring more artificial lighting, so brighter shades, especially on ceilings, can save energy. Structural color—hues created by refraction, as in Morpho butterfly wings and polar bear hair—is brighter than pigment and doesn't fade. For a Chicago bank lobby, designer Elva Rubio worked with biologists Janine Benyus and Dayna Baumeister to create a refractive ceiling that brightens the space without electricity, saving money, energy, and maintenance all at once.

According to Steven Chu, the U.S. Secretary of Energy, brightening the colors of all the roofs and pavement in the United States would slash emissions as much as banning all cars for eleven years, a staggering number. Art Rosenfeld, of the California Energy Commission, says that making all the world's roofs lighter could save the equivalent of 24 billion metric tons in CO_2 emissions. "That is what the whole world emitted last year," Rosenfeld has told the *New York Times*. "So, in a sense, it's like turning off the world for a year." On a summer day in the South, the temperature of a white roof can be 80 degrees lower than a black roof, and tests in Florida show that surface reflectivity alone can cut cooling costs 25 percent. Nationwide, light hues can save billions, making cities both visually and economically brighter.

But a generic approach to color would rob places of their distinction, for regional character and identity often are tied to palette. Think of the ochres of Tuscany, the red brick of New England, the gray shingles of Nantucket, the pastels of tropical islands, or the chalky white of the Greek Cycladic Islands, all of which are determined environmentally by the combination of local materials and response to light and climate. The tops of the earthen towers in the Yemeni village of Shabam are whitewashed to reflect heat. The black wool of Bedouin tents throws a deep, dark shade underneath, absorbs the sun's heat in the day, and reradiates it during cold nights, and the billowy white *thobe* worn by the Bedouins themselves reflects heat from the body. The red barn, an American icon, originally took its color from clay-based iron oxide pigments, as if it's painted with earth. The sky-blue ceilings of porches on Colonial houses are said to ward off spiders and wasps, who supposedly mistake it for the actual sky—visual insect repellent. Intelligent color choice can contribute to character, conservation, comfort, way finding, mood, maintenance, and financial savings all at once. So why is it missing from the standard toolkit of sustainable design?

Shaping Up

Hue is simply light of a specific wavelength, so color is light, and light is color. But what of the content of vision, the actual shape of what we see? Facing forward, our eyes collect images inside a nearly 180-degree field of vision, but those images are clearest within only 10 to 15 degrees, because the eye's receptors are densest in the middle, in the *fovea* ("arrow"), so we seek out the centers of things. Color, shape, and detail are most acute there. Psychologist

A. L. Yarbus, the first to track how eyes move over images, revealed just how much we look for clearly defined lines. Two eyes create depth perception, and the field of vision is designed for objects about twenty feet away; much closer, and the sightlines of the two eyes cross—hence "20/20" vision. Today, we spend most of our time in close quarters, which explains why eye strain has become so prominent. Other animals' eyes are set wide to scan whole environments, but we are designed to pinpoint targets and gauge distance, because our ancient ancestors chased after things rather than running away from them. We are hunters, with killer eyes.

Bilateral symmetry causes us to look for the same in the world. Our body image is so strong that amputees suffering from phantom-limb pain find relief after therapy in which the missing appendage appears in a mirror, because the brain wants to complete the body. Even the horizon is human. We draw it with our eyes from a handful of feet above the ground. The Romantic poet John Clare routinely went searching for the horizon and finally one day, after insanity set in, thought he found it. But it isn't out there—it's in here, in us. The Book of Genesis says God made man in God's image, but man remakes the world in his own image. Anthropomorphosis shapes everything.

Architectural historian Geoffrey Scott considered the "universal metaphor of the body, a language profoundly felt and universally understood," to be the foundation of architecture. "A metaphor," he wrote in *The Architecture of Humanism* (1924), "is, by definition, the transcription of one thing into terms of another, and . . . architectural art is the transcription of the body's states into the forms of building." We humanize the world by comparing it to our own bodies—what Germans call *Einfühlung*, "empathy." Top-heavy buildings feel off kilter, and we judge the scale of space in relation to our own size. Our awe in the face of sublime places—the Grand Canyon, the Great Plains, the Tetons, the Pacific Ocean—wells up because we feel tiny, insignificant, overwhelmed. An intimate place, by contrast, calms the sense of self, and the mechanics of such assurance are what Scott called "the laws of delight." Paris, long loved as one of the world's most beautiful cities, has one of the most consistent scales of any city. The heights of buildings conform to a reasonable distance for climbing stairs, typically five or six stories, so the character of Paris is shaped partly by the comforts of the human body.

In classical architecture, columns were conceived as bodies in stone, invitations to an embrace. At the Parthenon, the columns are tapered and the beams are bowed to compensate for perspective and appear truer to the eye. The proportions of the facade conform to a unique condition first identified

by Euclid, in 300 BC, as the "golden ratio"—divide a line into two segments so that the ratio of the overall line to the longer segment equals the ratio of the longer to the shorter. Subtract a square from a golden rectangle, and what remains is another golden rectangle, and so on and so on, ad infinitum.

These proportions occur seemingly everywhere in both nature and culture—in plants, shells, and crystals, and in the average shape of popular books, television sets, credit cards, and so forth. They provide the underlying structure for some of the most beloved designs in history—the face of the Mona Lisa, the bust of Nefertiti, the facade of Notre-Dame Cathedral, and the profiles of the Eames LCW Chair, the original iPod, and the Stradivarius. (Some even claim the proportions of the legendary violin are what give it its unique tone.) Astronomer Johannes Kepler called the ratio geometry's "precious jewel," and the golden rectangle's unique mathematical properties have led many to ascribe mystical origins to it, revering it as sacred, even divine. Is this simple shape, a little less than two-thirds as wide as it is long, handed down by God?

In tests conducted during the late nineteenth century, German psychologist Gustav Theodor Fechner, a pioneer of experimental aesthetics, studied a variety of rectangles to determine which are most preferred, and 76 percent of his subjects chose the ones whose proportions most matched the golden ratio. A century later, using modern, more accurate techniques, British researchers re-created the test with similar results. In 2007, neuroscientists at the University of Parma presented images of Classical and Renaissance sculptures with golden proportions to people with no training in art criticism. Some of the images were unaltered, while some were very subtly, almost indistinguishably distorted, and viewers repeatedly preferred the unaltered ones, which also stimulated more activity in parts of the brain associated with emotion.

"Golden" Rectangles.

This universally appealing ratio (about five by eight) has shaped some of the most popular designs in history, including Notre Dame, the Stradivarius violin, the Eames LCW Chair, and the original iPod. Recent studies show that the human eye takes in information more readily when viewing this shape.

What accounts for the consistent appeal of this geometry? Do we unconsciously perceive some kind of natural perfection in its proportions? In the 1960s, a group of American psychologists offered an intriguing explanation—that the golden rectangle relates to the area of the human visual field. Imagine drawing a rectangle within the borders of the image your eyes send to your brain; averaging these for a variety of subjects roughly produces a horizontal golden rectangle. This could explain why in 1925 Oskar Barnack insisted on the 3:2 aspect ratio (close to golden) for his invention, the 35mm camera. We prefer the shape, so the theory goes, because it most matches the frame around our picture of the world.

In 2009, Duke engineering professor Adrian Bejan may have resolved the ancient debate once and for all. According to his calculations, the human eyes can scan an image fastest when its shape is a golden rectangle. We take in information more efficiently when we survey the visual field horizontally rather than vertically, and physically the eyes move side to side more readily than up and down. Early humans, like gazelles on the open plain, had to track their terrain for potential threats, which were more likely to come from the side or behind, not from above. The more quickly animals can view their surroundings, the safer they are, and according to Bejan, "the shape of the image matters to how the image is perceived, understood and recorded."

Through mathematical analysis, Bejan found that for a given area the proportions most quickly scanned are the golden rectangle. For example, graphically it's the ideal layout of a paragraph of text, the one most conducive to reading and retention. Golden rectangles, declares Bejan, "emerge as part of an evolutionary phenomenon that facilitates the flow of information from the plane to the brain." This utterly simple geometric shape speeds up our ability to perceive the world. It reappears everywhere in culture because it aids our biological evolution—it helps us get smarter.

The View from You

Although the conscious mind digests images created by the two eyes together, unconsciously we react differently to the view from each eye separately. According to neuroscientists, the left hemisphere of the brain focuses on controlling well-established patterns of behavior, including language, while the right specializes in detecting and responding to novel stimuli, such as spatial relationships. Researchers at Washington University in St. Louis recently proposed that this division of labor evolved to give special attention to potential attack. Since motor skills in the left half of the body are governed by the right brain, this explains why, in lab experiments, even right-handed people respond more quickly to unexpected stimuli with their left hand (right hemisphere) than with the right.

The two halves also distinguish between global and local information, for the left brain analyzes specific details in the environment, while the right brain takes in the whole scene. What this means, say scientists, is that the left eye (right brain) is more prone to assess the total environment and look for unusual conditions. Could this be why research in retail settings finds that when entering a space people tend to move toward the right—so they can observe it more thoroughly with the left eye? Similarly, in a variety of popular buildings—Frank Lloyd Wright's houses, for example—the primary view often is encountered in this way. Could Wright have known innately how to reveal a view most dramatically?

How we scan the visual field closely relates to our instincts about space and place. In *The Experience of Landscape* (1975), Jay Appleton outlined the theory that our cultural, aesthetic, and spatial preferences are determined genetically. According to the Prospect/Refuge Theory, as he called it, we are drawn to environments that help us feel sheltered while still enjoying a clear view of our surroundings, where we can see but not be seen. The instinct is so ingrained, he claimed, that we seek these traits not only in the terrain but also in images such as landscape paintings.

Design can offer refuge at every scale—a wide veranda, a garden arbor, a window seat, a stone hearth, or a deep, wing-backed chair. Even whole cities and regions can offer such environmental assurances. Vancouver nestles where the North Coastal Range spills into the Strait of Georgia, where miles and miles of eroded coastline fold back on themselves to make a place riddled with inlets, coves, and myriad vistas. Seemingly every spot in the city—but particularly where the street grid shifts on the downtown peninsula—presents a protected place with a view of water and mountains. Long considered one of the world's most beautiful cities, Vancouver is a living model of Appleton's idea.

Home Is Where the Genome Is.
Acacia trees dominate the horizon on the African savanna, where the human species originated and spent the first 98 percent of its existence. Now people of all ages and cultures consistently choose acacia-like images as the most appealing, and studies show that viewing these figures can have physical, emotional, and mental benefits.

Prospect and refuge relate to the savanna hypothesis, the theory that wherever people go they look for Africa, specifically the rolling terrain, open vistas, and clustered trees of the Serengeti, our ancestral environment. Direct physical access to these features isn't necessary, since copious research confirms that just being within sight of green, growing things can improve productivity, health, and well-being. A Carnegie Mellon study linked seated views of windows to a 20-percent drop in "sick building syndrome" symptoms, including fatigue, neck and back pain, eye strain, headaches, and irritability. In a 2003 study of call centers, task performance jumped several percentage points among workers with views of vegetation, and at a Pennsylvania hospital, patients with garden views went home nearly a day earlier than those facing a brick wall.

What accounts for these benefits? Windows can evade the claustrophobia of closed spaces, but the very presence of an opening to the outdoors can't be the sole explanation, since some of the research compares different kinds of views. So the quality of light, movement, and patterns must be important. Yet, studies by environmental psychologist Judith Heerwagen and by Richard Coss and others show that even large photographs of natural scenes can produce similar results, lowering heart rate and blood pressure among stressed patients. If fixed, artificially lit images are effective, then light and movement can't be the only operative factors. There must be something important about the configuration of the view—that is, its shape.

The Fingerprints of Nature

In iconic nature scenes, one shape is ubiquitous: the tree. Based on evolutionary biology's findings about innate human preferences for savanna-like environments, Heerwagen and other psychologists have focused on tree images as signals of refuge that offer the potential for shelter, shade, and nourishment. Trees and other vegetation have inspired the art and architecture of every culture throughout history, which suggests their universal appeal. One species in particular, the *Acacia tortilis*, dominates the African savannah, where its silhouette emblazoned on the human retina for thousands of millennia, and research verifies that people are drawn to its shape—broad, spreading canopies and branches close to the ground. In a study by Coss and his colleagues, a diverse group of preschool children, regardless of nationality, background, or experience, consistently chose acacia-like trees as the most inviting, offering the greatest feelings of security. In a 2000 experiment conducted by Heerwagen and others for furniture manufacturer Herman Miller, people sitting at desks decorated with acacia images scored better in memory and problem-solving tests. So the acacia isn't just visually pleasing—it actually elicits a physiological response. What's so magical about this tree?

The appeal of the acacia in truth may have nothing to do with its being recognized as a tree. Experiments by psychologist James Wise and others used skin conductance techniques to measure anxiety during aptitude tests and found that participants exposed to highly abstract acacia-like images were less stressed than those who saw photographs of thick forest scenes. In other words, simplified diagrams of one kind of tree shape were more successful than realistic representations of another. Three significant revelations result from these findings: first, people respond not just to actual vegetation but also to related imagery; second, the imagery need not be realistic or recognizable as vegetation; third, not all vegetation or plantlike imagery works equally well. The implications for design are enormous. Plenty of research shows that access to natural scenes promotes well-being, but these other studies also suggest that nonrepresentational patterns can have a similar impact. In other words, abstract design can be good for you.

In fact, as the experiment above suggests, the right kind of artificial imagery can be better than the wrong kind of natural imagery. The common goal of offering building occupants views of nature could be overly broad, since certain scenes—dense forests or barren plains, for example—are not as effective as others. More and more evidence suggests that the operative feature of acacia-like imagery is not its overt expression of the savanna but, instead, its underlying order—the structure known as a *fractal*. Coined by French mathematician Benoit Mandelbrot in 1975, the term (meaning "broken" or "fractured") refers to irregular geometry that is continuously self-similar at

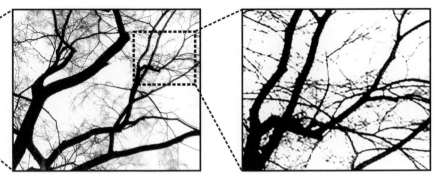

Natural Fractals.
These self-similar patterns appear everywhere in nature and have been called a "universal aesthetic" and the "fingerprints of nature."

every scale. The natural world is replete with fractals—in spinning galaxies and spitting sunbursts, in splitting crystals and splintering lungs, in creeping coastlines and veining leaves, in forking rivers and shivering snowflakes, and—importantly for human perception—in the explosive joy of a tree. Touching everything everywhere, fractals have been dubbed the "fingerprints of nature" and the "thumbprint of God."

Natural fractals are not those computer-generated paisleys, such as Mandelbrot's own, popularized in the late 1980s by James Gleick's book *Chaos*. Statistically generated to be precisely self-identical at different scales, these patterns appear mechanically repetitive, stiff, and artificial. Naturally occurring fractals, however, are self-similar, not self-identical, so they look looser, softer, less rigid and mechanical, and this fact could be exactly what makes them seem natural to the eye (and more structurally resilient in trees).

Mathematicians categorize fractals by their density (D) on a scale of 1 to 2, 1 being a flat line and 2 being complete fill; environmentally, the open ocean approximates D=1, while a thick jungle approaches D=2. Experiments by physicist Richard Taylor and others repeatedly reveal that a large majority of people (94 percent in Taylor's experiments) prefer a density around 1.3 or 1.4, which matches acacia- and savanna-like images, including the abstract diagrams from the Wise experiment. The theory is that a preference for these kinds of fractal images is genetically imprinted at a density we associate with the optimal environment for survival—too sparse means not enough sustenance, and too dense means not enough opportunity for surveillance. Using eye-tracking techniques, Taylor also has shown that we tend to scan our surroundings with a fractal pattern approximating the preferred density, even

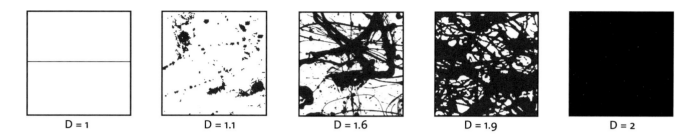

D = 1   D = 1.1   D = 1.6   D = 1.9   D = 2

when that pattern doesn't exist in the visual field. We seek out the desired imagery everywhere we look.

And not just in nature. Physicist J. C. Sprott has found that test subjects are invariably drawn to logarithmically produced figures called "strange attractors"—artificial images that look nothing like nature—if they conform to the same geometric characteristics of trees, clouds, and other natural fractals. And more and more studies are proving that some of the most lasting art, design, and architecture of various historic cultures the world over are fractal at the optimal density—oriental rugs, Islamic tiling, the "interior skies" of Persian domes, the Gothic tracery of Venetian palaces, housing patterns in the European villages, the Zen garden of Ryoanji in Kyoto.

Fractal Densities.

People are consistently drawn to patterns approximating D = 1.3, which can actually reduce stress.

> Some imagery isn't just visually appealing—it's
> also relaxing. Just looking at something can
> help you feel better.

The profile of a Doric temple entablature is nearly identical to the mathematical sequence known as "the Devil's Staircase." *Life* magazine named abstract expressionist Jackson Pollock "the greatest living painter in the United States" in 1949, when he was creating canvases now known to conform to the optimal fractal density. Taylor sees Pollock's late paintings as the culmination of a lifelong effort to excavate the images buried in all our brains.

Stylistically, the differences among the stately lines of a Greek temple, the spare serenity of a Zen garden, and the riotous drips and drabs of a Jackson Pollock couldn't be more pronounced, yet all of them display the organizing principles of natural systems, the geometry of life. In each of these cases, what evolved unconsciously over a lifetime or many generations of continual experimentation and refinement was a sensibility that can only be considered more *natural*. Fractals have been called a "universal aesthetic."

Again, such imagery isn't just appealing to the eye—it actually relaxes us. Taylor has shown that fractals at the optimal density can reduce stress levels by as much as 60 percent. Abstract visual patterns can cause a physiological reaction—we actually feel them in our bodies. Imagine the possibilities. If we can apply such imagery at any scale of design—graphics, clothing, carpet, walls, buildings, cities—we can design things that not only are more likely

> "Clouds are not spheres, mountains are not cones, coastlines are not circles. . . ."
>
> *–Benoit Mandelbrot*

Judge this book by its cover. The cover image mimics an optimal fractal pattern that physicist Richard Taylor has shown can significantly reduce stress—just by being in your field of vision. Studies by Texas A&M and others suggest that the green–yellow range of the color spectrum has wide appeal, through association with verdant landscapes and the promise of food.

to be enjoyed—they can help us feel better. The economic potential alone is momentous, since, as Taylor points out, the United States spends $300 billion a year dealing with stress-related illness. Just looking at something could help us all become healthier and wealthier.

Today many designers in various disciplines are experimenting with irregular patterning. Interface's popular "Entropy" line of carpet tiles, inspired by the disheveled look of leaves on a forest floor, revolutionized the industry by developing a way for every tile to be different. The versatility makes replacement easy, and the irregularity makes everyday wear and tear less visible, extending the life of the carpet as a kind of eco-camouflage. The potentially overwhelming scale of large buildings, such as the U.S. Census Bureau headquarters, can be humanized using such irregular patterns on their surfaces. The fractal-like screen on the facade of the Airspace Tokyo housing structure provides both shade and a forestlike view from the interior. Experiments with such treelike patterns applied to hospital windows show measurable benefits among patients. In *Fractal Cities*, Michael Batty and Paul Longley demonstrate that laying out a street network as a fractal tree can optimize density and linear frontage, thereby lowering unit costs and the total area of land needed. The gradual "organic evolution" of medieval towns shows similar economy and elegance, which is why, say Batty and Longley, the form of such places is often described as more "natural."

The Iconography of Habitability

Design can adopt nature's rules, patterns, and forms—its laws of shape. Half a century ago, in the final chapter of *The Death and Life of Great American Cities,* Jane Jacobs became the first to apply the emerging science of *organized complexity* to design. "What makes an evening primrose open when it does?" she asked, quoting mathematician Warren Weaver, a pioneer in the field. Weaver asked the question in 1948, Jacobs in 1961, and design and science are just now beginning to learn the geometric principles of organized complexity. Jacobs urged designers to adopt "new strategies for thinking," but new strategies for *shaping* are equally urgent. We'll need better knowledge and better tools to create things that are functionally and formally better suited to ecology. The geometry of complexity is the shape of ecology.

Yet, classical and modernist aesthetics both favor simpler, Euclidean shapes. "Geometrical figures are naturally more beautiful than irregular ones," according to Christopher Wren, architect of St. Paul's Cathedral in London. "The square, the circle are the most beautiful," Wren said, and philosophers, artists, and designers from Plato to Le Corbusier have agreed. But science doesn't. A growing body of literature attests to the instinctive appeal and resilient structure of subtler, more natural shapes. A disastrous failure of modernism was its blind faith in simplicity, and much of what people revile about many modernist buildings and cities is their blunt, inhumane, antiseptic forms.

"Why is geometry often called cold and dry?" asks Mandelbrot in *The Fractal Geometry of Nature.* "One reason lies in its inability to describe the shape of a cloud, a mountain, a coastline, or a tree. Clouds are not spheres, mountains are not cones, coastlines are not circles, and bark

Fractal Facade.

Airspace Tokyo, facade by Thom Faulders. Such patterns can be used on the facades of buildings to shade the interior, provide an appealing treelike view out, and create a more animated urban aesthetic.

Comfort in Irregularity.
SOM, U.S. Census Bureau Headquarters, Suitland, Maryland. Fractal-like patterns can be used to make very large buildings seem less imposing.

is not smooth, nor does lightning travel in a straight line." In the past, he recounts, mathematicians have tended to "flee from nature," disdaining its irregular, complex shapes as "pathological," a "gallery of monsters." Some fractals, marvels Mandelbrot, are "so oddly shaped that there are no good terms for them in either the sciences or the arts." By clinging to the overly simple, designers also have fled from nature. Euclid's compass can't capture God's thumbprint. Creating a "morphology of the 'amorphous,'" writes Mandelbrot, the geometry of complexity reveals "a totally new world of plastic beauty."

In their report for Herman Miller, Heerwagen and her team refer to images such as acacias and fractals as "Habitability Icons." Imagine an aesthetic founded on the iconography of habitability—a visual system based purely on nourishing mind, body, and soul. Natural aesthetics need not look overtly like nature, for instead of reproducing the pictorial image of vegetation, designers can learn from the principles and patterns of living forms. Can designers extrapolate the underlying order of life without losing its sensory appeal? Such an aesthetic could be at once groundbreaking and utterly grounded in nature.

Consider the strange attractor. In physics, an attractor is the condition toward which a system tends to evolve—a marble rolling in a round bowl, for example, eventually will come to rest at bottom center. The shape toward which a complex system evolves is a strange attractor. The movers and shakers of ecology, strange attractors shape much of nature—the dance of planets, the motion of oceans. Design can be such an attractor, a state of being toward which the world moves naturally—an accomplice to ecology. There are shapes and patterns that lure the human senses because they participate in larger forces unfolding over time, an eternal choreography not immediately detected but evident everywhere, all around us. With science and sensitivity, smart design can gracefully, beautifully tap into the abiding wonders and mysteries of the universe.

2008 Winner.

Jittasak Narknisorn, Positive Lounge Chair. The origami-inspired design bends a single sheet of material to cradle the body.

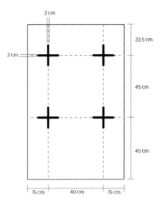

2010 Winner.

Eric Tong, Zpine Lounge. The honeycomb fiber structure has a high strength-to-weight ratio, contracts easily to allow compact shipping, and spreads into flexible, comfortable form.

One Good Chair. Organized by the author, the Sustainable Furnishings Council, and the World Market Center, the annual One Good Chair competition challenges young designers to use shape to save material and heighten comfort and joy.

6 | **The Animation**
of Everyday Things

Nothing gets made unless it is desirable.

—George Kubler

"NOKIA IS MAKING 13 PHONES EVERY SECOND," boasted executive Tero Ojanpera on the cover of *Fast Company* in late 2009. By the time you finish reading the next page, the company could spit out a thousand more.

More than ever before, our lives are stuffed with stuff, and manufacturers continue to pump up the volume. Every year, some 20,000 new consumer products—more than 50 a day—flood the marketplace, and since 1980 the number carried by a typical grocery store has more than tripled. In that same time period, reports the *New Yorker,* high-tech trademarks have grown from fewer than 10,000 to more than 300,000. According to consumer watcher

Sheena Iyengar, in 1994 there were half a million different consumer goods for sale in the United States, and now Amazon alone offers 24 million. Today, the average American buys more than fifty times as many products as the typical Chinese consumer does.

The growing number of things must mean that prosperity is growing too, right? Not necessarily. According to *Harper's*, 600 million people in India today have access to a mobile phone, though only half have access to a toilet. Here at home, Americans shop more than ever before and more than any other nation, various sources report, yet we save and invest less and less of our income, possibly because we consider an increasing number of consumer goods to be necessities instead of luxuries. A 2006 update to a regular Pew Research Center survey showed that the more people live with household products—everything from TVs to telephones to computers—the more they say they can't live without them. Twenty-five years ago, only 4 percent felt computers were essential, compared to 26 percent a decade ago and 51 percent today. In the 1990s, the Pew survey didn't even ask about cell phones because they weren't common yet, but now half of us consider them essential to our lives.

A 2009 poll asked one thousand people to review a list of some popular electronics and appliances—TV, computer, dishwasher, microwave, cell phone, and so forth—and decide which they would "give up to save the environment." Although a huge majority (83 percent) said they want to protect the environment, most wouldn't do so if it meant parting with any of those items. Only 8 percent would sacrifice their computers; 14 percent, their TVs; and 23 percent, their cell phones.

But the sheer volume and variety of the things we make are, quite literally, unnatural. In *The Evolution of Technology*, George Basalla compares the number of American patents (now over 6.5 million) to the number of known biological species (1.5 million documented) and concludes that the diversity of artificial things exceeds the diversity of living things by more than four times. Though Basalla marvels at the "richness" of technology, in actuality biodiversity protects life by ensuring survival through resilience, while technodiversity doesn't necessarily contribute much to the health and well-being of humanity.

People report that the more they shop, the less it satisfies them. This is not surprising, since consumerism can distract from other, more meaningful activities. Malls outnumber high schools, and we spend more time in them than we do in places of worship. Environmentalist David Suzuki cites an

Biodiversity and Technodiversity.

The number of artificial things (products) **(b)** exceeds the number of natural things (species) **(a)**.

extraordinary statistic: American parents spend six hours per week shopping and only 40 minutes playing with their kids. We buy more and enjoy it less.

It isn't just the act of shopping we don't enjoy—it's also the things we acquire. In *The Paradox of Choice: Why More Is Less,* sociologist Barry Schwartz explains that having *some* choice is good, but having *more* isn't always better, and unlimited choice can be extremely bad. Schwartz writes: "As the number of available choices increases, as it has in our consumer culture, the autonomy, control, and liberation this variety brings are powerful and positive. But as the number of choices keeps growing, negative aspects of having a multitude of options begin to appear. As the number of choices grows further, the negatives escalate until we become overloaded. At this point, choice no longer liberates, but debilitates. It might even be said to tyrannize."

Over the past few decades, the gross domestic product has risen steadily, but the number of Americans claiming to be "very happy" has fallen by 5 percent, or about 15 million people. During the same period, the number of products on the market has exploded, along with the incidence of clinical depression, now over ten times more prevalent than it was a century ago. As material wealth rises, mental health plummets.

Citing Nobel economist Amartya Sen, Schwartz suggests that "instead of being fetishistic about freedom of choice, we should ask ourselves whether it nourishes or deprives us, whether it makes us mobile or hems us in, whether it enhances self-respect or diminishes it, and whether it enables us to participate in our communities or prevents us from doing so." The foundational principles explored in the previous chapters can guide the design of consumer products that protect the planet but also satisfy us more. Picture a world populated only by essentials that nourish and enrich—inanimate objects that are more animated. If we could dramatically improve the effect that every physical thing has on our quality of life, we'd surely end up with fewer things. Environments large and small, public and private, would be shaped by neither excess nor scarcity but, instead, by a kind of elemental richness where everything is more fruitful and fulfilling.

> Picture a world populated only by essentials that nourish and enrich—inanimate objects that are more animated.

Long Life, Low Waste

"We just want to make great products," declared the late Steve Jobs, founder of Apple Computers. The huge success of Apple's iPod certainly counts as greatness by any conventional measure—technology, economics, marketing, culture, and, for many, personal lifestyle. (The colorful dancing-silhouette marketing campaign is as memorable as the product itself in its unabashed promise of liberation.) A 2004 BBC poll named iPod designer Jonathan Ive the most influential cultural figure in Great Britain—ahead of *Harry Potter* author J. K. Rowling, the most profitable novelist of all time. The iPod isn't a product—it's a revolution.

Apple may exist to make great products, but, as Jobs told NBC News, "If you always want the latest and greatest, then you have to buy a new iPod at least once a year." Greatness, it seems, has a short shelf life. "Apple introduces new, improved, smaller, faster, more powerful models that make their predecessors seem much less desirable," explains Giles Slade, author of *Made to Break: Technology and Obsolescence in America*. "This is what we call 'technological obsolescence.' Into this classic marketing strategy, Apple then adds 'planned' obsolescence. Lithium batteries sealed inside iPod bodies begin to lose their peak functionality after a year of use. By year two, you can only play your tunes half of the time. This makes the newest model your friend owns so much more attractive. Solution: Toss the old one into the trash and demand the newest iPod for Christmas, Hanukkah, or Kwanzaa. Apple, after all, was the company that originated the expression: 'Never trust a computer you can't throw out.'"

Throwing things out has meant big money for Apple, which has sold over 300 million iPods—about one every second—since introducing it a decade ago. In 2011, Apple made twice as much profit from phone sales as every other company *combined*. But planned obsolescence among manufacturers becomes learned impatience among consumers. A culture obsessed with newness creates a market based on disposability and an environment glutted with waste, because so-called "durable goods" aren't very. Every year, Americans get rid of over 300 million computers and electronics and recycle almost none. The flotsam and jetsam of cell phones make up almost half the total waste stream of high-tech trash, or "e-waste," the fastest growing category of garbage. About 80 percent gets shipped to Asia, almost all of it to China alone. China is where used gizmos go to die.

Ultimately, recycling doesn't completely solve the problem. In recovering a computer, for example, often only the metals are retrieved, while the energy-intensive circuitry and other materials are destroyed. Plus, recycling requires transporting the original materials again, and even the cleanest, safest, healthiest industrial methods can't prevent the harmful effects of shipping goods—the emissions of planes, trains, and trucks, the wear and tear on highways and roads, and the very need for more and more roads to accommodate growth. While any company can change its internal habits, not even the most environmentally committed can transform the entire transportation infrastructure. No, the problem may have less to do with the efficiency of production than it does with the frequency of it—not how we produce but how much and how often.

Making a computer can take some 80 percent of its total energy consumption, while using it accounts for only 20 percent, according to Eric Williams, coauthor of *Computers and the Environment*. Making a 2-gram memory chip requires 1,300 grams of fossil fuels and materials—650 times the resources. Nokia estimates that over 74 percent of a product's total energy usage and over 90 percent of its material waste occur during production—getting the materials, making the components, completing the assembly, and shipping to stores—while charging the batteries takes up about 25 percent of the total energy. This assumes a two-year life span, though the average is actually 18 months, which increases production-related energy to over 80 percent. Many sources even suggest that consumption during use is proportionally negligible, so better battery efficiency doesn't help much.

If the real impact of a product occurs during the industrial and not the consumer phases of its life, all we need to do is improve manufacturing methods and call it day, right? Not if we continue to dispose of things so quickly. The most wasteful thing about cell phones and other electronic gadgets is not how much energy we use to make them—it's how hastily we get rid of them. If you're the average person, every year and a half you replace your phone, and during your life you will have owned three dozen. Once you program in your contacts and learn all the new features, you start thinking about starting over.

Why? Does the old phone stop working? Does it get damaged, banged up, or lose its sheen? Or do you just get bored with it and want something new? Whatever the reason, how quickly we discard things shows how little we value them. The market encourages us to buy lots of stuff but replace it almost immediately, because the economy thrives on how much we buy, not on how much we use or enjoy the things we buy. In a consumer culture, everything is disposable, so we dispose of everything.

In that survey in which people said they wouldn't give up electronics to save the environment, all of the options to give up were generic, brandless products, except one—the iPod. Fewer than half (42 percent) said they would part with their iPods to aid the planet. Reactions to the survey, including those of the pollsters themselves, bemoaned the implication that consumers value the iPod more than they do the planet. Such loyalty, however, could be enormously beneficial to the environment.

As with other electronics, most of an iPod's impact—about 67 percent of emissions, according to Apple's 2011 reports—occurs prior to purchase, so its woefully short life is a tragedy. Clinging obsessively to your iPod would be wonderful if it were just the one iPod you refused to abandon. But people want *an* iPod, not necessarily the same one with which they started. Any iPod will do, and Apple encourages us to dump their product almost as soon as we buy it. What hurts the earth isn't that people won't give up their gadgets—it's that they will, and all too quickly.

Nokia estimates that prolonging the life expectancy of a phone by a year could cut its total energy consumption by more than 40 percent. According to Williams, continuing to use a computer can mean 20 times greater energy savings than recycling it: "Extending the life of a computer is the most effective way to reduce its environmental impact." Giving something a second life is a good idea, but continuing to use it in its first life is a better one—use it more so fewer are made. If this is true for electronic gadgets, consider the implications for everything else. Most consumer goods are inert, expending resources only during manufacturing and shipping, so for everything from bottles to bicycles and tables to tennis rackets, the conclusion is simple—the shorter the lifespan, the more wasteful the product. Longer life, lower waste. So how can design help prolong the lives of products?

Trash and Treasure

California's giant sequoia, which can grow to over 250 feet tall and 30 feet around, is the world's most massive tree—and one of the most breathtaking. Its famed beauty is one of the wonders of the West that helped ignite the American conservation movement. Yet, for a century following 1850, huge numbers were cut down, and entire groves were decimated, with little benefit. Because the wood is so brittle, three quarters of the tree shattered when felled, and the remainder was inappropriate for building, so often it was used for mundane purposes, such as toothpicks. That's the Industrial Revolution in a nutshell—three-thousand-year-old majesties torn asunder to dislodge meat from our teeth.

> "What things are cherished, and why, should become part of our knowledge of human beings. Yet it is surprising how little we know about what things mean to people. By and large social scientists have neglected a full investigation of the relationship between people and objects."
>
> —*Mihály Csíkszentmihályi*

It wasn't always this way. Many ancient and indigenous peoples consider an artifact as just one stage of an immortal substance, for design transforms living material without emptying it of life. Matter is alive, and everything is sacred. What the Greeks called *physis*, the true nature of a thing, the Lakota call *skan*. "Our ancestors spent their attention on handcrafted items," explains Scott Cloud Lee. "Things that are handcrafted with love have lots of skan in them; lots of medicine. Things that are factory made have . . . no love in them. Love is what directs skan. It is good to put our own energy into what we eat and use and wear. When people surround themselves with products that were largely made by 'fearful people,' they will absorb that fear." If we were to see every object as brimming over with life and love and channeling all of nature and humanity, we might hesitate to throw it away. Nothing is disposable when everything is your kin.

Of the countless things that are made today—everything bought and sold, borrowed or stolen, all products great and small—there are only two kinds: things we keep and things we don't. Some of them—swizzle sticks, cocktail napkins, bubblegum wrappers—we never really possess; we use them quickly, thoughtlessly, then cast them aside, barely paying any attention to our brief encounters with them. Others we own for a time because they pique our curiosity—trendy gadgets, fashionable shoes—but then we lose interest and send them on their way. Some, such as cars and furniture, might accompany us for years and decades, and some—photographs, jewelry, grandfather clocks—may stay with us all of our days.

Manufacturers and marketers spend a lot of money trying to understand why we buy these things, but they rarely investigate why we keep them. "To understand what people are and what they might become, one must understand what goes on between people and things," writes Mihály Csíkszentmihályi in *The Meaning of Things*. "What things are cherished, and why, should become part of our knowledge of human beings. Yet it is surprising how little we know about what things mean to people. By and large social scientists have neglected a full investigation of the relationship between people and objects." What makes us prize our most prized possessions? In the vast range of value between rubbish and riches, where are the lines dividing the objects we want for a while from those we cherish forever? Are things trapped in these categories, or can they move fluidly along the spectrum, shifting from novelty to keepsake to heirloom? Can one man's trash become the same man's treasure?

Durability might be a factor, of course, since it's easy enough to dump stuff when it falls apart. According to the automaker, 70 percent of all Land Rovers ever made are still on the road—after six decades. Panasonic claims its "Toughbook" mobile computers are ten times more reliable than standard laptops, 80 percent of which get replaced within three years, compared to only 15 percent of the Toughbooks. They're "designed to handle almost any situation," from the "bangs, bumps and spillage" of everyday use to "extreme conditions," such as heavy rain, dramatic temperature changes, and drops from heights.

In an economy of high-volume production, marketing for toughness seems a quaint throwback to a slower era. The Timex watch "takes a licking and keeps on ticking." Remember the old luggage commercial where a caged monkey mercilessly beats on a suitcase, with nary a dent or scratch? "Dear clumsy bell boys, brutal cab drivers, careless doormen, ruthless porters, savage baggage masters, and all butter-fingered luggage handlers all over the world. Have we got a suitcase for you." Do they still have a suitcase for the careless, ruthless, and savage among us? As apparently indestructible as those bags were, I don't know anyone who still carries one.

Durability doesn't guarantee longevity. A Twinkie might last forever, but who wants to eat it? Making a product tougher helps, but it doesn't stop the market from urging us to buy the "new and improved" version when it's released. Could brand loyalty give way to object loyalty? Can we make not only things that last but also things we love, things we want and will continue to want, things both durable and desirable?

In its mission "to make great products," Apple has learned a thing or two about generating desire. A 2007 Zogby International poll showed that Apple products are regarded to be as attractive as certain celebrities. Asked "who or what is sexier," 27 percent preferred actress Halle Berry, and 17 percent chose actress Scarlett Johanssen, while the iPhone tied with New York Yankee Derek Jeter for 6 percent of the vote. "Despite the adoration that its biggest fans hold for the device," Zogby concluded, "people still find other people more attractive." That the question would even be asked says a lot about Apple's success in the art of seduction.

British GQ editor Dylan Jones wrote a whole book about his obsession with Apple, and *iPod, Therefore I Am* is less design criticism than it is unbridled erotica: "The iPod has consumed my life like few things before it. It sits in my office, daring me to play with it, like some sort of sex toy. As well as being the greatest invention since, oh, that round thing that cars tend to have four of, or those thin slivers of bread that come in cellophane packets, the iPod is also obviously a thing of beauty. And I think I'm beginning to really fall in love. Seriously."

Durable and Desirable.

Julius Tarng, Modai concept phone.

"How can we lengthen and enhance the relationship between user and device?" asks Tarng. The front is nothing but interface, with playful graphics that adapt to the user's habits. The back exposes an easily removed interior module that can be upgraded without replacing the whole device.

Unfortunately, Jones's idolatry is fickle, more lust than love, since he doesn't covet one particular iPod. If he listens to Apple's advice, he'll spurn his annually and find a younger object of his affection, and by now he'll have done so several times since deserting the one that served as muse for his 2005 book. Apple's strategies of obsolescence foil any long-term commitments and doom the bond between customer and product to be short-lived—more summer fling than significant other. The company creates products people want but can't keep, and a love that won't last is heartbreaking.

Could you ever tire of a thing whose appearance regularly changes to suit your pleasure?

But it isn't just the functionality of Apple's products that fails. The Jonathan Ive look banks on the image of purity, untarnished and unblemished, and of course it fades with age. The instant your iPod gets nicked or scratched, the nubile fantasy spoils, so its intentionally short life is both an economic strategy and an aesthetic necessity. The iPhone suggests a more promising way to continue captivating its users. With its razor-thin edging and generous screen size, it's more interface than object—hardware whose image is determined almost exclusively by software. Programming requires no manufacturing or shipping, so if the machinery lasted, its aesthetic could be updated continually—just download a new look.

"For us," Ive says of Apple, "it is all about refining and refining until it seems like there's nothing between the user and the content they are interacting with." Yves Béhar sought the same in the $75 XO-3 and the XOXO computer, which are practically frameless, buttonless tablets: "The media or content on the computer will be the prime visual element." Each release of the operating system and every new application offer an opportunity to change not just the utility but also the basic appearance of the phone. If these products adopted Panasonic's toughness engineering, they could become virtually indestructible and endlessly adaptable. Could you ever tire of a thing whose appearance regularly changes to suit your pleasure?

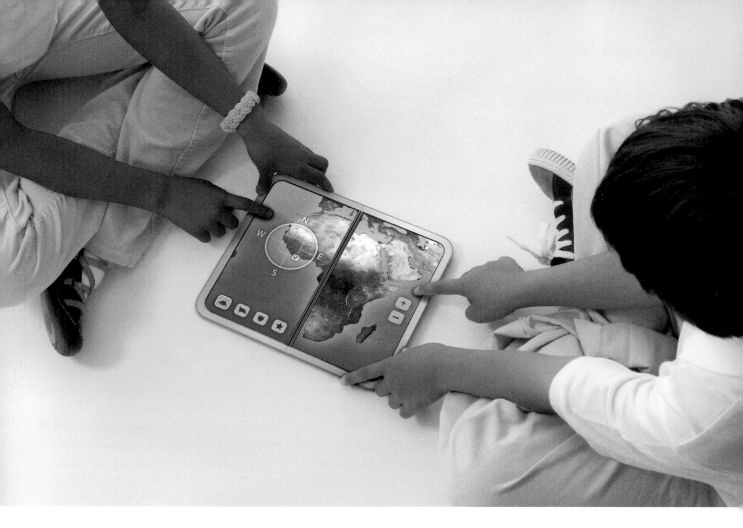

The Perfect Product

Designers long have fantasized about a perfect product that cleans itself, heals itself, and never breaks—a maintenance-free object. Old standbys like the cast iron skillet actually get better with age, their surfaces toughening up as they oxidize, and high-tech materials such as shape-memory alloys and self-healing polymers may realize the dream of eternal youth. Nokia's "Morph" concept phone proposes state-of-the-art nanomaterials mimicking the strength, flexibility, and durability of spider silk, shape-shifting to adapt to each task at a cellular level.

But the fantasy of flawlessness could be misguided. "The perfect is the enemy of the good," warned Voltaire, and the good should concern sensory pleasure as much as sturdiness. The Japanese art of Wabi Sabi finds beauty

An Experience, Not an Object.
Fuseproject, One Laptop Per Child, XOXO.
The soft but razor-thin edge and generous, collaborative screen invite a more direct relationship with information—software unencumbered by hardware. More image than object, it suggests a new kind of product, whose aesthetic could be continually freshened up by downloading a new look.

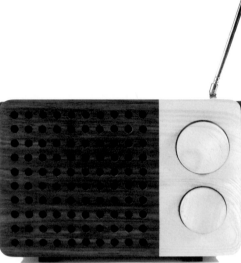

The Perfect and the Imperfect.
(a) The Nokia Morph phone is self-cleaning, self-preserving, and physically and aesthetically flexible. *(b)* Areaware's wooden Magno Radio celebrates the need for care: "Its uncoated surface should be oiled periodically to encourage a deeper connection between user and object."

in the imperfect—the frayed and the faded, expressions of natural cycles of growth and decay. This morning a local restaurant served me fish tacos on a palm leaf plate. Made from naturally discarded sheaths of Adaka palm tree leaves collected from the forest floor, the plates are biodegradable and compostable, but they're also a joy to hold. Rough and thick, with irregular veins and folds, every plate is different, its texture irresistible to the touch, like Grandma's hands. How can that much comfort come from a disposable dish? A far cry from the Styrofoam clamshell you don't think twice about tossing out.

We can become emotionally attached to something not in spite of its wear and tear but, in fact, because of it. Acts of maintenance—polishing the silver or winding the clock—can create meaningful bonds, which is why we call this "caring" for something. We take solace in the familiarity of an old shoe, a faded quilt, a deformed hat. Evidence of time shows us we're not alone in our own aging; we're mortal, and so are our things, which offer the comfort of companionship.

All matter succumbs to entropy, the inevitable process of slowing and breaking down, but this is only natural. There is a relationship between entropy and empathy, and sentimental affection can be directly proportional to physical deterioration: if you love something, its material condition is immaterial. A young girl I know clung to her cherished stuffed dog, "Pups," until it disintegrated into little more than a hunk of shaggy brown fur. A college friend had dragged around a stuffed animal that began life as some kind of rabbit but had long since lost its extremities and facial features, and by the time I met it the creature was unrecognizable as any particular species. It was simply "Reggie."

Can product designers learn how to inspire such devotion? Can a cell phone create the Reggie Effect? Could a laptop mimic the tender appeal of a Bahamian cotton doll whose skirt is stitched with the entreaty "Please Open Your Heart"? If an iPod emulated a Teddy bear (the iPooh?), churn-dependent Apple might go bankrupt, unless it altered its business model by creating lifelong partners instead of annual customers, by resurrecting the lifetime guarantee to ensure attachment as well as functionality and service.

To captivate consumers longer, designers will need a better understanding of what stimulates emotional longevity. When we examine the life of an object, there are three basic considerations, what I call the Three Orders of Green. The first and most familiar to environmentalists concerns a product's internal composition—chemical content, material ingredients, and assembly. Call this the product's *anatomy*. The second order concerns a product's life cycles—where it comes from and where it's going. This is the product's *biography*, a genealogy of its sources, supply chains, manufacturing processes, shipping, reclamation, reuse, and so forth. Together, the anatomy and biography of a product tell us much about its effects on human and ecological health.

This information is essential, but it overlooks another dimension. The past and future of an object are key, but what of its present, the here and now? Biography charts an object's condition over time, but equally important, if not more so, is its presence at any given point in time. The life *of* a product is one thing, but what of life *with* a product?

Consider this third, less familiar order to be the product's *ecology*. While anatomy considers the internal relationships between the parts and pieces, and biography represents a product's vertical relationship with time, ecology views a product's horizontal relationships with people, places, and other things—how it's used, what experiences it elicits, the meanings it evokes, and its cultural and natural settings. The first two orders directly affect health, while the third also can influence well-being. Anatomy is *composition*, biography is *continuity*, and ecology is *context*.

Although typical green standards are getting better about the composition and continuity of products by improving material chemistry and process efficiency, these standards by and large have yet to embrace or even acknowledge aesthetics, personal relevance, and natural and cultural context as critical components of sustainable product design. The oversight of context is understandable since, by definition, things mass-produced for a global market defy local conditions. In addition to the consumption represented by overproduction and long-distance transportation, an inevitable challenge with global products, which are most things made, is their detachment from particular cultures and places. Once upon a time, all the earmarks of culture—architecture, furniture, clothing, cuisine, language—were drawn from local conditions and ingredients. In an age of worldwide markets, how much room is there for regional products?

Product Placement

The unspoken myth about design is that consumer products occur in isolation. Googling the word *product* yields 6 billion hits, mostly (like many of the illustrations in this chapter) images of things floating in white space—empty chairs, readerless books, riderless bicycles, roadless cars. Designers often envision objects that exist in worlds of their own, but nature abhors a vacuum. Everything has context, and meaning is impossible without it. Bring together an object and a place, and both inevitably change—they look, feel, and act differently.

There may be a relationship between the growing number of products and our increasing disconnection from place, since the objects may not be creating meaningful connections to our lives. We Americans may think we need more and more of the fifty new products introduced daily, but for fifty thousand years, the indigenous communities of Australia have thrived primarily with three simple tools—the spear, the digging stick, and the boomerang. Some might call Aboriginal technology unsophisticated, but which is better adapted for survival—these "primitive" tools, which have helped sustain a people for fifty millennia, or the countless gadgets that come and go, accessories to a nation that over the second of its brief two centuries has become ten times more depressed? "The astonishing endurance of the Aboriginal peoples must be attributed, at least partially, to their minimal involvement with technologies," writes David Abram in *The Spell of the Sensuous.* "Their relation to the sustaining landscape was direct and intimate, unencumbered by unnecessary mediations. They relied upon only the simplest of tools . . .

and thus avoided dependence on specialized resources while maintaining the greatest possible mobility in the face of climatic changes."

A marvel of aerodynamics, the boomerang—possibly the first gravity-resistant invention, a Stone Age flying machine—embodies its landscape. Flinging far and wide, a "throwstick" speaks of flat plains and open space and could not have evolved in the clutter of deep forests or the slopes of steep mountains. Its shape is tuned by the cooperation of body and environment, of hand and land. The boomerang exemplifies the coevolution of people, places, and things. If sustainability refers to the enduring harmony of culture and nature, the Aboriginal kinship with the land must stand as one of humanity's shining examples.

The best designs, like the boomerang, gracefully connect us with our worlds—our stuff unites our selves with our surroundings. Consider your clothing. On the one hand, what we wear directly expresses how we relate to the world. We use attire to navigate weather and climate, bulking up in the winter and the north and slimming down in the summer and the south, so our wardrobes signal the seasons as well as our surroundings. The Middle Eastern *sari* and the South Pacific *sarong* are simple fabrics that can be worn in various ways to keep the wearer cool in hot, humid climes. Some of the most common apparels have lost histories tied to place. Nineteenth-century British soldiers in India curbed casualties by dying their tunics a muddy tan to blend into the background. Using an Urdu word for "dusty," they called it *khaki*. One hundred fifty years later, Old Navy and the Gap have made khaki a staple of casual attire.

Often, clothing has little to do with comfort or context. All over the globe, many customs—everything from tribal neck rings to corsets and stiletto heels—take a serious toll on the body. What passes for fashion can be painful, both physically and visually, imposed by fleeting global fads, not local needs. The Paris runway overshadows your backyard. The very idea of "sustainable fashion" sounds self-contradictory, like "timeless trend." What happens when fashion goes out of fashion? How can we make things that last in an industry driven by novelty?

Eco-fashion leader Kate Fletcher speaks of "fast" and "slow" clothing, wearables that either wear *out* or wear *in*. In an article titled "Clothes That Connect," she writes that diverse clothing products "sustain our sense of ourselves as human beings; they are heterogeneous and user-specific and recognize a wide range of symbolic and material needs. . . . Homogenization and autonomy are eschewed in favour of expressiveness and difference. Diverse fashion grows out of an individual or a particular place."

Some high-tech methods now can create high-touch products and accomplish the kind of mass diversity Fletcher describes. Whole garment technology, such as Issey Miyake's A-POC ("A Piece Of Cloth") line, allows designers to produce an entire item of clothing directly on the knitting machine, simultaneously molding the fit to the wearer and avoiding scraps of waste—tailoring without a needle and thread. Many designers are experimenting with modular garments, piecing them together from standardized parts, like Legos of fabric. Mixing and matching in one garment can extend the life of the outfit by allowing repair on small segments, like a puzzle whose pieces can be infinitely rearranged.

Creatures of Comfort

Smart products are shaped to use materials intelligently (Conservation), fit the body (Attraction), and embrace place (Connection), but many products fail to accomplish any one, much less all, of these aims. Think of chairs. You might believe that objects intended to be sat upon would also be designed for comfort, but often they are not. Many are meant mostly to convey social and political power—the queen's throne, the bishop's *cathedra*, the overstuffed leather seat of the "chairman" of the board. The most popular designer chairs often reflect only the designers' capricious interests. Classic modern pieces, such as Mies van der Rohe's Barcelona chair and Marcel Breuer's Wassily chair, which he called his "most mechanical" and "least cozy" work, demand effort simply to climb in and out of them. And their materials and weight make them extremely energy intensive to produce and ship.

Some recent chairs are more thoughtful. Emeco's 20-06 chair, designed by John Small, answers the question, "How slender can a chair be and still retain its strength?" An update on the classic 10-06 Navy chair, its spare shape shaves 15 percent of aluminum off the original, stacks ten high, and weighs seven pounds. Konstantin Grcic's MYTO chair minimizes material and maximizes support by revising the modernist cantilever chair in high-tech plastic. For his Bone chair, Joris Laarman employed software that mimics skeletal growth. Beginning with the weight and stresses of a typical chair, the program creates a bonelike structure that puts material only where it's needed to support the body properly. Like a computerized Michelangelo, it carves the optimal form out of a block of digital stuff.

Even a perfectly efficient structure doesn't ensure comfort, however, and an inherent problem with manufactured furniture is the challenge of satisfying everyone. Mass production is for the masses, and even chairs designed around advanced ergonomic principles aren't fail-safe, since the science of ergonomics is based on statistical averages, not individual bodies.

Customization is smarter. Tokujin Yoshioka's diaphanous Honey-Pop chair is uniquely molded by the individual user. A flat sandwich of thin but strong honeycomb paper expands to a voluminous mass that adapts to your body, taking on what Yoshioka calls "shape without a shape." The act of sitting molds the chair, like a gorgeous, gossamer bean bag. Using digital body-scanning techniques, manufacturing could incorporate such precise tailoring in volume production. Neri Oxman designed her shaping-shifting chaise lounge, "Beast," to respond automatically to the body's subtle movements, as described by *Interview* magazine: "Imagine a chair that moves when you move, that adjusts to every muscle in your body, that responds like a living organism . . . a chair kind of like a really excellent lover."

Nevertheless, fitting the form of the body and providing comfort are not necessarily the same thing, partly because the very idea of comfort is elusive and subjective. Galen Cranz, author of *The Chair: Rethinking Culture, Body, and Design,* explains that the word *comfort* has come to suggest "ease," while the original meaning of the Latin root was "strength." The modern use of the term implies relieving effort, whereas the older version, which she recommends designers rediscover, referred to building long-term health and well-being. Comparing furniture design to the principles of alternative movement practices such as the Alexander Technique, Cranz finds most chairs woefully lacking. Over time, even many of the most ergonomic designs teach the body to be weak because we learn to rely on the chair instead of our own muscles, and prolonged use actually deforms the physique and creates ailments by restricting the flow of blood and oxygen.

Cranz points out that sitting is harder on the body than standing is. Pressure on the spinal discs is 30 percent greater when we're seated, resulting in strain to the spinal column, back muscles, lower back nerves, and diaphragm. According to sick-leave statistics Cranz cites, musculoskeletal problems among administrative workers are higher than in any other industrial sector, so sitting can be risky business. The same research found a far lower incidence of injury among populations of those parts of Africa and Asia where it's customary to squat, not sit.

Because of these facts, Cranz believes that the best chair is no chair at all—crouching or resting on the floor is preferable. Nevertheless, she recognizes that how we recline often relates more to culture than to physiology, so she suggests ways to "reform" the Western chair. First, because no two people are alike, every chair should be adaptable to different body shapes and sizes. The height, depth, width, and seat and back angles all should adjust readily to any position. Second, because furniture should encourage the body to support itself, Cranz recommends backless chairs such as stools or benches in order to build torso strength. Third, the chair should allow constant motion. "People are designed for movement—we want our weight to shift constantly to avoid over-taxing one set of muscles," she says. "The static, mechanical fix is not the answer." A chair should rock and roll.

> "The shape of things we use can engender not only better living, but also better human behavior."
>
> *—Akiko Busch*

With these modifications in mind, Cranz advocates certain alternatives. The inflatable therapy ball, first used in yoga and other movement practices, has become popular among some office workers, even while being ridiculed by others. But its spherical form accommodates many angles and heights, as well as movement and self-support, and because it's inflatable and lightweight, it's easy and efficient to manufacture and ship. Kneeling chairs curve the knees under in order to keep the spine in its natural position and promote blood flow through gentle movement. Cranz calls Peter Opsvik's Balans chair, for example, "certainly the most radical of the twentieth-century and probably since the invention of the chair-throne itself," five thousand years ago.

You Are What You Eat With

Designs for eating are just as challenging as designs for seating, and the most popular "green" utensils often are unpleasant and uncomfortable. In 2011, the U.S. House of Representatives stirred up controversy by replacing the congressional commissary's biodegradable cups and utensils with traditional plasticware made from petroleum—in large part because the greener alternatives were uncomfortable and dysfunctional. Forks bent easily and spoons softened in soup.

As the *Washington Post* put it: "The cutlery seemed to start composting early. Like in the middle of lunch." The new mandate was simple: "Find cutlery that held their shape." When supposedly more "responsible" choices can't hold their shape, they get thrown out.

If we expect them to be used, the things we make must be more than efficient and durable—they have to inspire comfort, joy, even compassion. In *The Uncommon Life of Common Objects,* her reverie on the romance of physical possessions, Akiko Busch recounts how an entire line of kitchen utensils resulted from one man's compassion for his wife. Retired OXO founder Sam Farber might not have realized the inelegance of many standard kitchen tools if he hadn't noticed his arthritic wife struggle with a potato peeler while they were cooking together one evening. The conventional, thin-steel peeler, prone to rusting and awkward to wield, hadn't changed much in a hundred years. Farber's designers studied the variety of gestures and motions people use with cutlery, and from this subtle choreography came several essential changes. The larger, oval-shaped, rubber handle of the "Good Grips" vegetable peeler improves leverage, control, and slippage, and flexible fins adapt the grip to the individual. But the larger proportions also *look* more grippable, as if inviting us to take hold.

Busch believes the Good Grips peeler reflects a basic truth about design: "The shape of things we use, these ordinary kitchen utensils like potato peelers and cucumber slicers, can engender not only better living, but also better human behavior. When you think of it this way, it makes all the sense in the

Shaped for Grabbing.

(a) Karin Eriksson's Gripp Glasses are elegant and easy to hold, even for the physically impaired. **(b)** In response to his daughter's struggles with polio, Yoshiro Aoyagi developed the Willassist shape-memory utensils, which adapt to the form of every hand.

world that the OXO vegetable peeler came into being because a man wanted to help his wife." The result, says Busch, was "an act of kindness disguised as a kitchen accessory." Similarly, Yoshiro Aoyagi developed a set of shape-memory utensils in response to his daughter's struggles with polio. The pliable handle of his spoon, for example, shifts its shape to fit the unique form of any hand. For Busch, these aren't tools so much as "small agents of human decency."

Kitchen utensils have special significance, says Busch, because we associate them with sustenance: "I wonder if it is because these are hand-held objects that we use to prepare food—and by extension to nurture and sustain ourselves—that we are willing to attribute near-human qualities to them. It seems inevitable that such items, almost in spite of themselves, are instruments not simply of food preparation, but of human behavior, coordinates that can help us calibrate our places in human relations."

In *Near A Thousand Tables,* his history of dining, Felipe Fernández-Armesto remarks that no activity connects people to their environment more than taking a meal: "Our most intimate contact with nature occurs when we eat it." As the vehicles of this contact, utensils shape the degree and character of its intimacy. Reportedly 30 percent of the world eats with knife and fork, 30 percent with chopsticks, and the other 40 by hand. Upon first thought, eating by hand would seem the most "intimate" among these traditions, since nothing comes between you and the food. And think of the material and energy to be saved if those who prefer utensils—all 4 billion of us—enjoyed the taste of our own fingers more than we do the taste of metal or wood.

With knife and fork, all that slicing and stabbing seems not so much intimate as it does impolite. (When forks first appeared in England in the early seventeenth century, reports one source, they were ridiculed as frivolous: "Why should a person need a fork when God had given him hands?") Food historian Margaret Vissor recounts that Western table manners evolved to discourage violence and even cannibalism: "Behind every rule of table etiquette lurks the determination of each person present to be a diner, not a dish." In 1669, the French banished pointed knives from table settings to avert murder during meals.

Chopsticks, or *kuàizi* (Mandarin for "quick little fellows," with "chop" being English slang for "quick"), predate the Western fork by four thousand years. Unlike the knife, which is confined to the kitchen in Asian cultures, chopsticks suggest a kind of civil restraint, an atmosphere of mutual respect, not shared fear, among diners. Simple stalks of wood or bamboo, traditionally fashioned by hand, not fired in forges, chopsticks are significantly more resource efficient than metal cutlery, and the manual dexterity required to brandish them strengthens the hand, but socially and culturally their true value may be in the reverence they engender for the bounty of a feast. Does the third of the world raised on them experience a more "intimate contact" with nature than those of us who brandish knives at the table?

The Good Grips slogan, "tools you hold on to," aptly expresses how important tactility is for comfort and longevity. Things we want to grasp are less likely to leave our grasp. Would that every product fit like a glove, or a worn leather baseball mitt. In the end, the most sensible, sensual, and sustainable design strategy might be to create things that are a joy to hold, behold, and hold onto. There is an art and a science to making the weight and heft of a glass or bowl or spoon feel right in the hand. A thing with balance instills great pleasure but also inspires deep respect.

I know a teacher whose first lesson with her Montessori preschool is always the deceptively simple act of carrying a bowl across a room, "ever so beautifully." To watch toddlers revel in the delight and responsibility of caressing their vessels while carefully measuring each step across the floor is a delight in itself. If from such an early age every one of us learned to treat every object as if were sacred, over a single generation many of the earth's problems might gradually, naturally, just fade away. Ever so beautifully.

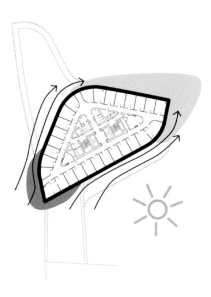

Shaped by Place.

Sauerbruch Hutton, KFW Westarkade, Frankfurt, Germany. A four-story podium follows the street, while the ten-story tower above follows the sun, wind, and views to optimize heat gain, ventilation, and comfort, making this one of the world's most energy-efficient office buildings.

7 | The Architecture of Difference

Belief in the significance of architecture is premised on the notion that we are, for better or for worse, different people in different places.

—Alain de Botton

"WHY do some buildings arouse in us feelings of happiness or excitement or repose?" asks Grant Hildebrand in *The Origins of Architectural Pleasure.* "What is it in them that elicits pleasure? . . . [A]re there any characteristics we can identify that seem to improve our chances of contentment?" Hildebrand argues that shared environmental instincts evolved into common archetypes of architecture, which he calls "the aesthetics of survival."

Architect Michael Benedikt summarizes the basis for such aesthetics: "Architecture, which we usually take to begin in earnest some nine thousand years BC, represents no more than one five-hundredth of the time mammals have been extant. During this seminal period, the essential elements of advantage accorded by certain patterns—figures—of shelter construction and site selection were becoming a part of *all* living and surviving." Among these significant patterns, Benedikt counts places of shelter and surveillance, defensible places, places high and low, light and dark, near and far, inside and out, cold and warm. Their enticement, he claims, is "no less reliable than any natural physical law."

Architecture embodies humanity's relationship with the earth.

Could these attributes become the foundation for a systematized method of design—an architecture of attraction? The preceding chapters outlined a set of principles for the aesthetics of ecology, and this chapter applies these ideas to the shape of places. In its various functions—everything from primal shelter to symbolic expression—architecture embodies humanity's relationship with the earth. Because certain patterns of form and space have appeared consistently in many cultures over time, arguably they must have some special appeal and might constitute a universal vocabulary, a "natural physical law" of building.

Studying the canon of widely revered works of architecture and urbanism, Christopher Alexander has spent a lifetime developing the premise that a timeless "pattern language" positively shapes the environment. His classic book *A Pattern Language* is a practical guide to 253 basic building blocks of great places—a well-defined entrance, deeply carved openings, contrast of light and shade, the compelling passage from one space to another, and so on. Because they are based on empirical observation, Alexander declares these conclusions to be purely objective—a matter of fact, not opinion. They constitute not just a method but a mandate for design.

Alexander's magnum opus, the four-volume *The Nature of Order*, is the culmination of four decades of research, thought, and experience. Studying thousands of examples from nature and design, Alexander identifies the shared traits of all things beautiful—a tulip leaf, a leaping cheetah, a lily pond, ripples on the pond's surface. A Norwegian barn door, a Persian bowl, a Shaker cabinet. A giraffe's coat, a Ghiordes prayer rug, a Shinto shrine. The Doge's Palace in Venice, Venice itself, a Matisse, a butterfly, a human face. All of these, in Alexander's eye, share fifteen fundamental properties of form, scale, composition, hierarchy, variety, contrast, and context that, added up, bring things to life, or *Life*, with a capital *L*, as he calls it. Whether or not the thing in question is literally alive, it conveys "an eerie magic essence that *feels* alive." Alexander aims to pin down this "eerie essence" by discerning exactly which qualities enhance and express life—that is, he means to dissect magic.

The Meaning of "Life"

In *A Theory of Architecture*, Nikos Salingaros expands on Alexander's ideas by rationalizing design as a "scientific problem." *Structural order*, or coherent composition, is governed by "a set of rules that are akin to the laws of physics." Drawing on a breadth of knowledge from biology, neurology, geometry, mathematics, physiology, psychology, and information theory, Salingaros outlines which shapes the eye seeks out when it scans the field of vision, which patterns most aid comprehension, why differing scales of form feel cohesive or not, and so forth. What makes us feel connected to our surroundings, he claims, can be explained mathematically. In what he deems "a totally innovative approach to design," Salingaros compares visual preferences to thermodynamics by outlining a series of "intrinsic, computable values" any building can incorporate. How a building feels relates to how it's formed, and form is just geometry and mathematical patterns.

Adopting Alexander's terminology, Salingaros lists guidelines for how to design buildings with a high degree of *architectural Life*, based on the prevalence of certain characteristics in successful buildings throughout history. This prevalence, Salingaros insists, suggests that these qualities satisfy "a profound innate need in human beings." In his comparative index of twenty-five famous structures, ranked by their degree of "Life," the Taj Mahal and the Moorish palace of the Alhambra, in Spain, rank the highest because they combine compelling form and rich detail. No building after the year 1900 scores very well because of the relative lack of detail—for Salingaros, modernism's rejection of ornament and color was also a rejection of instinctive human appeal.

The most audacious part of Salingaros's scoring is how he does it. Delivering on his promise of a scientific method, he goes so far as to translate *Life* into a simple mathematical formula:

$$L = T \times H$$

Life equals the product of *Temperature* (smaller-scale traits, such as color, density, detail, and contrast) and *Harmony* (larger-scale organization). Each is the sum of five clear principles that are easily identified and evaluated, then graded on a scale of one to ten, so a building with perfect *Life* would achieve a score of 100. The Alhambra and Taj Mahal each score a 90, while some of the most revered examples of nineteenth-century architecture rank in the 50s and some icons of the twentieth century barely earn any points at all. Some contemporary architects might dismiss Salingaros as overly nostalgic. However, whether or not you completely agree with the results, the method itself is captivating—like architectural alchemy, it scientifically analyzes the meaning of Life. With his unprecedented technique, Salingaros demystifies design by transforming aesthetics into algebra.

> If aesthetic appeal can be mathematically calculated, quality can be quantified, and pleasure can be measured.

Salingaros's comparison between aesthetics and thermodynamics is more accurate than he might think, since the features he admires can play both visual and environmental roles. Traditional features, such as eaves and arches, cornices and arcades, recesses and overhangs, shed rain or provide shade that appeals to both the eye and the skin, and these cooling effects can enhance the performance of a building. Variety and detail often are smarter than none. Although it's true that modernist architecture typically lacks these details, a traditional visual style isn't necessary to provide the aesthetic and environmental benefits of traditional features. In fact, the brilliance of Salingaros's method is that theoretically it can inform design in any vocabulary, incorporating time-honored principles within even the most innovative forms.

The implications for sustainable design are considerable. When visual appeal can be expressed numerically, it can be verified just like any other standard of green. Quality can be quantified, pleasure can be measured. If such methods can guide design to improve comfort and well-being—and therefore promote long-term value and preservation—with results that are easily calculated, what prevents them from becoming a common part of green practice?

Six Kinds of Style

In a break from convention, Salingaros intentionally ignores floor plans because a building's layout "is not directly perceivable to the user." He also rejects the modernist distinction between form and surface as an intellectual conceit that has no bearing on how people actually relate to buildings. As he sees it, our sensory mechanisms respond to all visual information regardless, so he concentrates only on "the immediate impressions of elevations and surfaces from a human viewpoint." In other words, he's interested in *style*.

Of course, he doesn't use that term—designers and critics alike shy away from it because it smacks of superficiality. Fifty years ago, architectural historian Siegfried Giedion wrote: "Today, the moment we fence architecture in within a notion of 'style' we open the door to a purely formalistic approach [which has] about the same effect on the history of art as a bulldozer upon a flower garden. Everything becomes flattened into nothingness, and the underlying roots are destroyed." At that time, Giedion was right to be concerned about modernism's devolvement into "pure formalism," but today sustainable design risks the opposite, a devaluation of form. Since our first and often lasting impression of something comes from its looks, style isn't shallow.

But where does it come from? Understanding what determines the form and image of any building can help explain green buildings better. I can identify six kinds of architectural style in three categories. These are not mutually exclusive, and many examples fit several categories, but generally every work of architecture ever built, anywhere in the world, conforms to one or more of these fundamentally different attitudes toward design.

Market-Based Form

Market-based form, which includes Corporate Style and Populist Style, feeds off economic influences. Image-making is a business strategy, and style is what sells. As the backbone of suburban sprawl, market-based form is good for profit but not always good for people or place.

Corporate Style, which dominates suburban public space, treats buildings as commercial advertising—shape as branding. A fast-food restaurant is a three-dimensional logo whose main selling point is that we readily identify it with the company—the McDonald's Mansard hut, Taco Bell's faux-adobe

MARKET-BASED FORM

Corporate Style

Populist Style

HISTORY-BASED FORM

Personal Style

Epochal Style

PLACE-BASED FORM

Regional Style

Circumstantial Style

Style Matters. Every work of architecture relates to six basic styles, representing different attitudes toward the purpose of design. Only two are consistent with the goals of sustainability.

villa, Der Wienerschnitzel's Alpine A-frame, Bob Evans' broken pediment, and White Castle's white castle. To evoke a mood, if only vaguely, corporations co-opt architectural features associated with particular regions. Detached from their original context, each of these stolen icons now represents a business, not a time, place, or people. Culture gives way to commerce in these billboard buildings. If, as Schiller mused, architecture is frozen music, the suburban strip is a cold commercial jingle.

Populist Style defines suburban private space through production housing—shape for the mass market. Whereas Corporate images create market distinction, Populist images define the average market. Forty or fifty years ago, American Populist Style was the Cape Cod, thirty years ago it was the Ranch house, and now it's the McMansion—bloated, propped-up manors with gables piled upon gables. Cookie-cutter houses aren't designed, they're dressed up—in Mediterranean, French country, or neo-Colonial costumes, or some murky mix of them all. Like Corporate Style, Populist Style plucks these images away from their origins, distorts them, and plops them down wherever people might buy them. Coast to coast and border to border, the same houses turn communities into commodities. The high-brow version of Populist Style—New Urbanism—offers more variety and better-quality construction, but it still treats every place the same, as if spilled from the grab bag of architectural history.

History-Based Form

History-based form, which includes Personal Style and Epochal Style, proposes that design rises out of special historical figures and forces. One strain of this view, the "Great Man" theory, holds that "the history of the world is but the biography of great men," in the words of Thomas Carlyle. The other strain, the Zeitgeist theory, was best summed up by art historian Heinrich Wölfflin: "Different times give birth to different art." Both the Spirit of the Age and the Spirit of the Sage describe history and design as the story of extraordinary people and events.

Personal Style, the most coveted among architects, is set by the individual preferences of the designer—shape as taste. Like Corporate Style, Personal Style is a form of branding, but instead of advertising the owner, it advertises the architect. Modern architectural history is a chronicle of Personal Style—pick up any trade magazine, academic journal, or design monograph from the past several decades, and seemingly every structure featured is an example. The most celebrated designers all practice it, because history equates the consistent vocabulary of a Frank Gehry with maturity and mastery of the medium. Of course, the individual interests of the designer do not always represent the best interests of the community, and Personal Style turns the city into the artist's canvas—the space of private expression, not public fulfillment. We allow the architect alone to judge what's good, because we anoint him (rarely her) with what sociologist Max Weber called "charismatic authority," power lent to leaders for their exceptional character. "Hero worship" is another way of putting it.

Epochal Style proposes that there is an appropriate language for an era—shape as a sign of the times. The German modernist Mies van der Rohe considered this the very definition of architecture, "the will of an epoch translated into space." As the argument goes, every Zeitgeist has a *Zeitstil*, the "style of the age." Modernism is an obvious example, as Le Corbusier made clear in 1923: "Our epoch is fixing its own style day by day. It is there under our eyes." Henry-Russell Hitchcock and Philip Johnson fixed its name too, in the title of their book, *The International Style* (1932): "Today a single new style has come into existence.... This contemporary style, which exists throughout the world, is unified and inclusive, not fragmentary and contradictory." By definition, the International Style renounced local flavor in favor of the global taste. While the best examples, like those of every era, transcended polemics and continue to find new relevance every generation, the mediocre examples now are dismissed as "period pieces," and the worst disappeared within a generation. Mies practiced for half a century, beginning in 1920s Weimar Germany and ending in 1960s Corporate America, his *Zeitstil* still intact. He turned the Epochal into the Personal.

Place-Based Form

Place-based form, which includes Regional Style and Circumstantial Style, embodies the unique conditions of its locale. Its purpose is ecological in that it supports and signifies the relationships between culture and nature in a given context.

Regional Style considers what's appropriate for the larger context—shape for setting. Regional architecture speaks in a local tongue: Nantucket's wind-weathered saltboxes on the sea, Arizona's extrusions of the earth, the snow-laden peaks of Swiss chalets, the gray granite streetscapes of the Scottish highlands, the bright colors and light shutters of the colonial Tropics. Location is only one factor, as critic Lewis Mumford explained in 1941: "Regionalism is not a matter of using the most available local material, or of copying some simple form of construction that our ancestors used. . . . Regional forms are those which most closely meet the actual conditions of life and which most fully succeed in making a people feel at home in their environment; they do not merely utilize the soil but they reflect the current conditions of culture in the region." Take the Japanese *shoji* house. The deep, tapered eaves and thin paper screens tell of an atmosphere heavy with moisture, while the obsessive order and exacting detail reveal a society heavy with ritual. Regional character grows out of many people living in and shaping a place over long periods of time.

Circumstantial Style, possibly the rarest type, responds to a project's unique conditions—shape for situation. A tailored approach to people and place, it molds design around the fine grain of a site, its use, and its users. Where Regional Style is a generalization of context, Circumstantial Style is highly specific and localized and may bear little resemblance to other buildings in the area—or anywhere else. Frank Lloyd Wright's Fallingwater may be the most familiar example of the Circumstantial approach. Precisely shaped to its wooded shelf above a stream, this house couldn't move ten feet without spoiling its effect. Yet, because Wright's work is so self-referential and his personality so large, the specificity of Fallingwater is difficult to digest now—like Mona Lisa's smile, its image can't escape its status as a cultural icon. A clearer example is the Casa Malaparte, its stepped red wedge knitted to a rocky outcropping overlooking the Gulf of Salerno on the Isle of Capri, Italy. After firing his architect, the owner, exiled journalist Curzio Malaparte, solicited the help of local stonemasons and built the house himself, producing a one-of-a-kind design unassociated with any architect's oeuvre—custom made from a broken mold.

Monday-Morning Architects

Which of the previous six styles are best suited for sustainable design? Green means to enliven the intersections of culture and nature and enhance the long-term well-being of people and place. Ultimately, this longevity takes precedence over individuals, corporations, markets, and fads, so at its heart sustainability is *apersonal* and *atemporal*, meaning it is communal and timeless. Architecture is rarely a solely private concern, because buildings aren't just part of the public realm—they *define* the public realm. As such, standards of architectural aesthetics and value are best judged by entire cultures over many generations.

The first four architectural styles all are vulnerable to self-interests and fleeting trends: Corporate Style embodies commercialism, Personal Style represents individualism, Populist Style aims to please the market but fails to embrace place, and the Epochal is trapped in the moment. (In the words of opera conductor August Everding: "Whoever marries the Zeitgeist will be a widower soon.") Consequently, the only types fully consistent with the aims of sustainability are the two remaining styles, the Regional and the Circumstantial. Green architecture should embody a beauty born of its place—the sense of its terrain, the sensibilities of its people.

In *Nightlands: Nordic Building,* Norwegian architecture historian Christian Norberg-Schulz beautifully explains the differences between the light, space, and culture of north and south. "Here in the North, the sun does not rise to the zenith but grazes things obliquely and dissolves in an interplay of light and shadow. . . . In the North we occupy a world of moods, of shifting nuances, of never-resting forces, even when the light is withdrawn and filtered through an overcast sky." The character of Nordic light fundamentally differs from the stable, single-mood environment of the Mediterranean, writes Norberg-Schulz: "Hence the extensity of southern space: sun saturated and homogeneously whole, it is limited only by the horizon and the vaulted sky. The morning brings the emergence of space, the evening its withdrawal, but with the sun directly overhead, space reveals itself as it in reality is."

The beauty of the Alhambra arises in great part from the local climate. Wonderfully proportioned courtyards, reflecting pools, deep colonnades, and ornamental tracery together shape a comforting place by creating shade, capturing breezes, cooling the air, and softening sunlight. The Alhambra's architectural "Life," unrivaled in Salingaros's estimation (though he makes no mention of climate or context), shows an extraordinarily deep sympathy for setting. Life and place are bound together.

In nature, imagery and ecology are interwoven, and the aesthetic of a living thing emerges from and often echoes its surrounds. The golden coat of the lioness blends in with scorched Serengeti grasslands; the spotted leopard, with the dappled shade of the jungle. The polar bear is white; the grizzly, brown. Fish are bright in the belly—seen from below, they blend with the sky beyond—but they're dark on top, to disappear in the deep. In the hot, wet rain forest, plants grow large fleshy leaves to drink in light and breathe out the damp; in the thin air of the mountaintop, spiky needles evade overexposure. These are natural models for Regionalism—distinct forms generated by general differences of climate and context. The Circumstantial also has its precedent in nature. Sunflowers follow the light; moss finds the shade. Pacific seawinds sculpt the Monterey cypress, and a pine projecting from a cliff in the Rockies bends like macaroni. Alone in a field, an oak forms a thick, round canopy; in dense woods, it stretches straight. These creatures adapt to what's around them. Life is a shape-shifter.

Vernacular architecture acts this way too. The compact box of the New England Colonial holds its heat in winter, its roof pitch sheds snow, and its sparing windows dissuade drafts. A Virginia dog trot is the opposite, lying low and yawning in the middle to breathe in the breeze. Thai houses wear woven skins and tiptoe with stilts on soft terrain. Cycladic houses of the Aegean islands are dressed in chalky white to reflect heat and stay cool. The Persian windcatcher (*badgir*) reaches for the sky, fingering the breeze and pulling hot air up from below. Chinese dwellings in the silt belt of the Honan area are carved into the earth to stay warm in winter and cool in summer. Roof forms alone vary dramatically from place to place—flat when hot and dry, pitched when cold, deep eaves when wet. The roof is the architectural equivalent of what biologists call a *homology*, a similarity between features, such as a beak or a talon, that have adapted to distinct contexts. Different forms for different places.

Asked about stylistic consistency, Mies van der Rohe famously replied that an architect can't create a new architecture "every Monday morning." But why not, especially if every week she finds herself building in a different place for different people with different purposes? Each project offers possibilities for invention within its individual conditions. As commercialism threatens to rid the world of diversity, a vital role for design is to create highly customized buildings diligently adapted to the unique circumstances of people and place. We need more Monday-morning architects.

The Physics of Beauty

Barcelona residents call Antonio Gaudí's Casa Mila *El Pedrera*, "the rock quarry." Layered into its undulating, clifflike surfaces are traceries of metalwork and tile mimicking marine life—fish scales, seaweed, shells, and

Regional Form.

(a) Lake/Flato's World Birding Center in Mission, Texas, adapts the regional vernacular of ~~r~~ural structures in the Lower Rio Grande Valley. *(b)* The sweeping lines of Bohlin Cywinski Jackson's Ballard Library in Seattle, Washington, stem from the neighborhood's Scandinavian and maritime history.

snails—and colorful chimneystacks glisten on the roofscape like serpents rising from the surf. This aesthetic is more than the fanciful expression of a wild-eyed architect—it ties his work directly to the local culture. The phrase *mar y muntanya*—"sea and mountain"—captures the unique blend of flavors in Spain's Catalan region. Local cuisine, such as the popular *paella*, combines meat and fish—game from the mountains and shellfish from the sea—and the most familiar Catalan architecture is a stew of geological and biological imagery.

The culinary analogy is apt. Architectural historian Peter Collins recounts that behind the original notion of *taste*—both aesthetic and gustatory—was a basic desire to please the consumer, a value that has all but disappeared in contemporary architecture, which tends to develop around the designer's individuality. But, as Collins put it, to emphasize personal expression is like judging an omelet by the chef's passion for breaking eggs.

Ambitious contemporary architects often see Regionalism as a hindrance to innovation, the shackle of the past when they crave the freedom of the future. But many modern examples show that Regionalism not only accommodates but encourages inventive expression. The Finnish architect Alvar Aalto's entire career attested to the power of innovation within tradition. His fascination with the dialogue between clean lines and rough textures modernized rustic Scandinavian traditions, tempered by a love of nature. "The profoundest feature of architecture," he wrote, "is a variety and growth reminiscent of natural life. . . . In the end, this is the only real style in architecture."

Today, the inspiration of Aalto is evident—intellectually, if not stylistically—in Rick Joy's sculpted houses of rammed earth in Arizona, Miller Hull's pared-down Pacific Northwest lodge look, and Lake/Flato's streamlined Texas prairie buildings. The sweeping lines of the Ballard Library in Seattle, Washington, stem from the neighborhood's Scandinavian and maritime history. In Australia, Glenn Murcutt's work plays ingeniously with both Regional and Circumstantial form. In many of his houses, stilt structures, operable walls, and sculpted roof forms are lessons learned from vernacular traditions that evolved to suit Down Under climes, while the scoop-shaped canopy of the Southern Highlands House deflects the southwest wind whipping across the open plain, a unique response to unique site.

> "The physics of beauty is one department of natural science still in the Dark Ages."
>
> —*Aldo Leopold*

The Regional responds to macroclimate and culture—how high the sun goes, when the rain falls, how hot and cold it gets, how thick the air feels, the textures of materials, the taste of local craft. For their exquisite Gamble House (1909) in Pasadena, California, Greene & Greene employed local craftsmen and materials for the incomparable woodwork, a symphony of oak, redwood, fir, and cedar. In an uncharacteristically serious moment, humorist Sarah Vowell has spoken of the Gamble House in moral terms: "The warmth of the place is comforting, but the craftsmanship of the carpentry makes me want to be a better person." Working within local traditions brought the house in ahead of schedule and under budget, while Frank Lloyd Wright's houses during the same period were notorious for doing the opposite.

The Circumstantial reacts to microclimate and the immediate context: the size, shape, and slope of the land, eddies of breezes, watersheds, viewsheds, the light through the trees, the shade of a neighbor, the bend in a river. Seattle architect James Cutler shows a deep respect for the land by knitting many of his houses into the existing shape of the site to avoid altering the grade or removing a single tree. KieranTimberlake composed the striated facade of the Loblolly House by literally drawing on top of a photograph of the pine trees in the background. The result blurs the lines between structure and setting.

Whether a building adopts the Regional or the Circumstantial—or both—can depend on its purpose in the community. Like an organism in an ecosystem, its form is fired by its position in a place. Conservationist Aldo Leopold called this "the physics of beauty," as he describes in *A Sand County Almanac*: "The physics of beauty is one department of natural science still in the Dark Ages. Not even the manipulators of bent space have tried to solve its equations. Everybody knows, for example, that the autumn landscape in the north woods is the land, plus a red maple, plus a ruffled grouse. In terms of conventional physics, the grouse represents only a millionth of either the mass or the energy of an acre. Yet subtract the grouse and the whole thing is dead. An enormous amount of some kind of motive power has been lost."

Just as the grouse's role in the woods cannot be fathomed by measuring its mass, a building's full environmental impact cannot be completely understood solely through the volume of resources it consumes. To reduce green building to a hollow list of material quantities robs architecture of its own kind of "motive power." Green building conserves energy, optimizes its ecological footprint, and improves performance. Green architecture, however, becomes an integral part of its community by embracing the total environment, a wedding of natural and cultural values.

The three players in Leopold's north woods—maples, grouse, and land—have brethren in the built environment as well. Fabric, the equivalent of maples in the autumn landscape, gives a place its basic shape—the mansarded housing blocks of Paris, for example. A Figure, an architectural grouse, is a specially shaped structure commanding attention—the Eiffel Tower, the Capitol in Washington, the birdlike Milwaukee Art Museum. Fabric and Figures dwell in the larger natural context—San Francisco's hills, the Seine, the Potomac, Lake Michigan. Fabric defines the general character of an environment, and Figures provide the accents. Balance is key—too much fabric, not enough focus; too many figures, not enough coherence. It's been said that a street lined with all the great buildings of the past would be a very bad street with great buildings. The whole must exceed the sum.

Every great place at every scale is formed by the vibrant interplay among Figures, Fabric, and land. The Duomo set against the terra cotta roofscape of Florence, nestled in the Tuscan hills with the Arno snaking through. The

Perpendicular Gothic spires of Cambridge's Kings College Chapel struck against the low dormitories, flat yard, and gentle River Cam. The lotus-bud towers of Angkor Wat rising from the temple galleries in the thick Cambodian jungle. The Rotunda commanding the Lawn, spilling toward the Blue Ridge Mountains, at the University of Virginia.

Fabric buildings tend to house the most common functions—offices, housing, retail—whereas Figure buildings typically are special civic or cultural uses, such as capitols, museums, libraries, and worship centers. The uses of Fabric buildings often change over time; Figures often do not. A commercial office building can switch owners every few decades and tenants every few years; by contrast, the Louvre has been a museum for half a millennium. To ensure their continuing viability, a key strategy with Fabric buildings is designing for flexibility, so they may facilitate any number of purposes over time. Think of cast iron loft buildings in Manhattan's SoHo district—their open plans, large windows, and tall ceilings allowed them to evolve through many uses. The Uffizi Museum in Florence originally housed offices (*uffizi*), but its narrow spaces and large windows wrapping a courtyard made it perfectly suitable for an art gallery. Versatility spurs adaptation and preserves the heritage of a community.

Circumstantial Form.

KieranTimberlake, Loblolly House, Taylors Island, Maryland. The striated cladding reflects the pattern of pine trees surrounding the house.

Because of their special role in communities, Figure buildings offer special opportunities for innovation. The cultural significance of a museum or a capitol demands all the creativity designers can summon, and the aspiration of such buildings should be nothing short of the perfect marriage of economy and ecology—through zealous conservation of resources and diligent adaptation to place.

Regional and Circumstantial Form.
Glenn Murcutt,
House in Southern Highlands,
New South Wales, Australia.
The proportions echo vernacular and indigenous building traditions, and the scoop-shaped canopy deflects the southwest wind whipping across the open plain.

These exceptional structures can signal the most progressive understandings of how people and place interact.

Together, Fabric and Figure strike a balance between tradition and innovation. Because the bulk of a community often is composed of Fabric buildings, Regional form is the most logical and respectful choice—the Fabric of a great place is woven from threads spun in that place. Because Figural buildings are less common, they can afford to vary from the prevalent vocabulary while still respecting it, and Circumstantial form provides the greatest opportunity for experimentation within the context of its surroundings. Whether Regional Fabric or Circumstantial Figure, the most responsive work marries functional flexibility with a specific context to strengthen the natural and cultural character of its setting.

Adaptation and Invention

In some ways, the principles behind an aesthetics of ecology differ markedly from many of the most influential ideas of modern architecture. Le Corbusier favored simple geometry and praised primary solids—cubes, cones, spheres, cylinders, pyramids—for their purity and clarity: "It is for that reason that these are *beautiful forms, the most beautiful forms.* Everybody is agreed as to that, the child, the savage and the metaphysician." Although Le Corbusier reiterates a very old opinion going back at least to Pythagoras, whether "everybody" agrees is debatable, since studies show that people consistently are drawn to nature's more complex patterns, which our animal brains associate with sustenance and survival. Primary geometry rarely occurs in the visible universe of biology and physics. Even apparent spheres are rarely actual spheres—the earth, moon, and sun all bulge in the middle, shaped by spins, orbits, and the tugs of other worlds. The stuff of pure mathematics, Le Corbusier's "beautiful forms" may be the metaphysician's ideal but not necessarily that of the child or the "savage"—or the ecologist.

Similarly, although Louis Sullivan borrowed the phrase "form follows function"—a staple of modern architectural theory—from nineteenth-century biological theory, the idea reflected an inaccurate view of nature. (Darwin showed that in natural selection, morphology occurs randomly and remains only if it ensures survival, so form and function are more give-and-take than they are cause-and-effect.) Independently of its origins in science, fitting form to function implies efficiency, but often modernist construction in fact was and is highly inefficient. Standard structural members (columns, beams, studs, and so forth) typically are oversized and poorly shaped. The rectangle, the most common shape in construction, is inherently clumsy at carrying weight and stress (and in the case of mechanical ducts, for conveying air). We build in straight lines and right angles not to enhance performance but simply because production techniques such as metal extrusion favor simple forms. In this sense, the modernist edict should have been "form follows *industry*."

Although green architects reject the mechanical inefficiency of modern architecture by emphasizing passive cooling and heating, most green buildings still conform to conventional construction techniques. Since World War II, construction has relied increasingly on standardization in order to lower costs, but at the expense of material conservation. For example, the staple of contemporary residential and commercial construction alike—stud-wall framing—only marginally improves on balloon- and platform-framing techniques developed in the nineteenth century. Wood framing is wasteful throughout the entirety of its life cycle—from tree harvesting to lumber production to standardized dimensioning to construction and eventual demolition. The "stick-built" house remains an archaic form that flourishes only because of familiarity and habit.

Fitting form more specifically to place requires more innovative methods, with two basic options: adapt existing techniques or invent new ones. *Adaptation* applies novel approaches to conventional materials and methods. For instance, some materials, such as dimensioned lumber and plywood, come in specific sizes and shapes, so using them responsibly means working with these predetermined forms. Techniques such as digital fabrication and computer-aided manufacturing are redefining the relationship between design and construction, yet, so far, these techniques have been used most notably to accommodate artistic vision, not necessarily to conserve resources. But these methods can be applied to produce dramatically more intelligent designs.

For example, as an alternative to the typical stud-wall framing system, architect Sean Dorsy has developed an expandable wall system that is significantly more efficient with materials through sourcing, design, and application all at once. Because plywood is rotary sawn (cut from the circumference of the log), it wastes less wood than dimensioned lumber such as two-by-

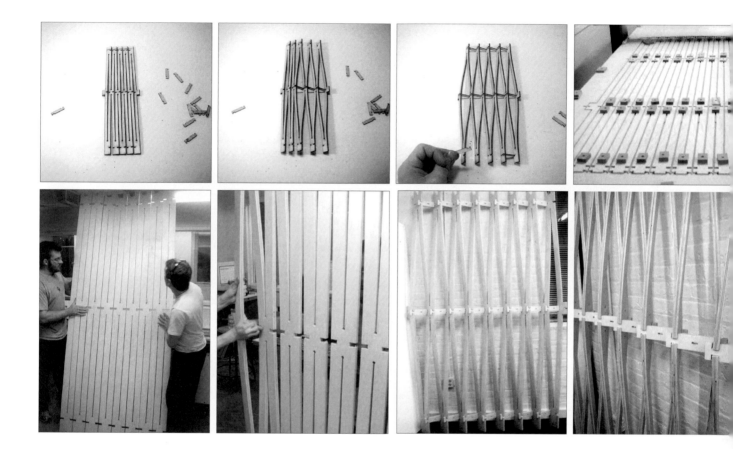

fours. Through digital fabrication, Dorsy saves every inch of standard four-by-eight sheets, leaving nothing behind on the shop floor. He unfolds the plywood to create an amazingly durable, origami-like frame that can be used as the innards of a partition or as an open room divider. Held together with clips instead of nails, it can be taken apart easily and redeployed, making it cheaper, lighter, stronger, more versatile, and more attractive than stud framing.

A second type of innovation, *Invention*, proposes altogether new methods. Some materials, such as concrete, are amorphous prior to fabrication, so they do not have predetermined form and thus offer tremendous flexibility. The limiting factor with concrete is not the material itself but the way it's installed, because the form is determined by the formwork,

A Wall like an Accordion.

Sean Dorsy, Expandable Wall System.
The system unfolds a sheet of plywood to make a wall that is lighter, stronger, cheaper, more durable, and more efficient than a typical two-by-four stud-frame wall.

the boxes into which the mix is poured. But lightweight, flexible textile molds can achieve shapes that are at once more complex and cheaper and easier to assemble. Experimenting with fabric forms, Mark West and his students at the University of Manitoba could revolutionize concrete construction.

For any given structural component, such as a beam, stress and strain are not consistent along its length. Yet, beams in both concrete and steel tend to be built as continuous sections sized around the worst-case scenario (the most demanding load). From a strictly environmental point of view, this is unnecessary and wasteful, because optimal performance requires varying the beam's shape in every dimension. West's fabric-formed beams solve this problem. Like an animal skeleton, material goes only where it is needed, using three hundred times less weight in formwork material and half the concrete of an equivalent rectangular beam. West calls it "net shape fabrication." The resulting porpoise-like form is both super-efficient and breathtakingly beautiful. With such methods, form finally does follow function.

Self-Sustaining Form

What if we applied the examples of the accordion wall or the porpoise beam to every part of a building or even to entire building shapes? If each beam, column, floor, wall, window, and roof were shaped with the ingenuity of West's concrete or Dorsy's plywood, what could construction become? What would an architecture of such dramatic innovation look like?

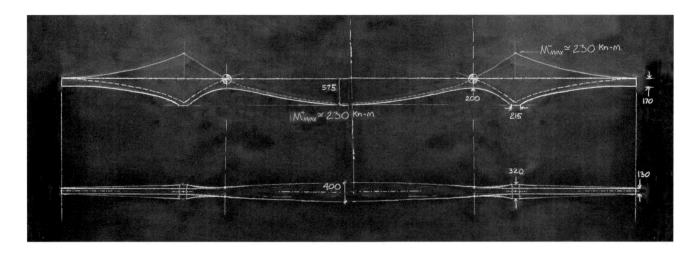

A Beam like a Porpoise.

Mark West et al., University of Manitoba, experimental concrete beam.

Fabric-forming uses three hundred times less weight in formwork material and half the concrete of an equivalent rectangular beam—material only where it's needed.

The possibility isn't new. Nearly two centuries ago, after running out of brick (and funds to purchase more) during the construction of the University of Virginia, Jefferson used inventive form to reduce material and increase strength in his famous serpentine garden walls. The undulating shape—the only part of the entire campus design not derived from Jefferson's beloved neoclassical precedents—required only one layer of brick instead of the typical two and therefore saved some 40 percent in material. Limited resources propelled innovation.

Likewise, while the architecture of Gaudí often is seen merely as expressive skin wrapping simplistic bones, in actuality his understanding of geometry was visionary. The columns of the Sagrada Familia, for example, twist simple geometric solids into treelike shapes that employ relatively little material to carry a heavy load—a tour de force of structural design and expressive joy. Neither Jefferson nor Gaudí typically is characterized as "green," and their inspired examples seem to have escaped the notice of ecologically minded designers today.

The product of such techniques might be called *self-sustaining form*—geometry that enhances structural and material integrity through the conservation of resources. Buckminster Fuller's famed geodesic domes are tiled, or "tessellated," with a hexagonal pattern commonly found in the looser formation of soap bubbles, honeycombs, crystals, and cracks in the earth, the 120-degree angle often being the path of least resistance and greatest stability. Fulfilling an ancient fantasy of idealizing the physical world, Fuller was able to transform a building into pure geometry by enclosing maximum volume with minimal surface and mass. "How much does your building weigh?" he was fond of asking—as if architecture could become so diaphanous that it might float away.

The vision of weightlessness is nearly realized in Grimshaw's EDEN project, a vast series of domed botanical gardens in Cornwall, England. Eight interwoven spheres built of lightweight-steel, icosahedral space-frames are clad in air-filled super-insulated foil (ETFE) weighing less than 1 percent of the same volume of glass. Ganged into transparent "pillows," the foil gives the structure a buoyant image, as if balloons gently drifted onto the site. Shigeru Ban's Japanese Pavilion at the 2000 Hannover Expo pushes the possibility of ephemeral architecture even further. A paper sheath around a paper-tube structure, it is a Japanese lantern to EDEN's high-tech balloon. Building it was simple—a diagonal lattice grid of tubes was laid flat on a series of scaffolds and simply pressed together with mechanical jacks. The domes took shape naturally as their ends secured in place. Instant architecture.

As architecture becomes more enmeshed with its place, it takes on subtler forms.

The profile of the Hannover structures is not a semicircle but a catenary, the curve formed naturally by any flexible line shaped by its own weight—a vine in a jungle, moss on a branch. (The word itself means "chain.") Structurally, a catenary, or funicular, is the optimal geometry for any load-bearing arch because it conveys force more efficiently than a regular arc. The deceptively simple example of the catenary demonstrates the inadequacy of theoretical ideals and primary geometry for making a more ecological architecture. Unlike the philosophically perfect Platonic form, by definition the catenary can be understood only through how it interacts with an environment—fix the ends and let nature do the rest. Just add gravity.

The catenary fascinated Gaudí, who incorporated it into many structures, and the shape has long been a fixture in the building traditions of various indigenous peoples all over the world. The Inuit igloo, the wigwam of the North American Plains Indians, the Zulu "beehive" house, and the Toda hut of Southern India are all catenary domes or vaults. The seemingly simple igloo is a complicated affair of spiral-stacked blocks of ice. While the igloo and wigwam are similar in form, they use very different materials to deal with

opposite challenges of climate—heavy mass to preserve heat in the one, hide or bark to adjust to dramatic temperature swings in the other. But in each case, their shape uses little material and surface to bring comfort in an extreme climate.

Although some contemporary examples, such as the Hannover Pavilion, apply modern technology to ancient wisdom, they lack the inspired Regional adaptation of those older forms. Vernacular architecture tunes

Place-Based Efficiency.

Foster + Partners, City Hall, London.

Combining state-of-the-art material efficiency and site-specific design, the building leans into the sun, shading itself and gathering light onto the riverwalk below. Soft curves diminish wind loads on the surface and air turbulence at the pedestrian level. The result requires no mechanical cooling and uses only a quarter of the energy and 75 percent of the surface area of a conventional building.

harmoniously with its place, but many so-called "eco-tech" buildings appear generic, high in sophistication but low in relevance. Fuller planned identical versions of his dome for many different locales, and the ETFE super-structure is becoming a high-tech staple. Virtuoso acts of material conservation, these clone domes could occur nearly anywhere and so represent the economy of means divorced from the ecology of place. Because geometry alone drives the form, it fails to adapt more specifically to its context. Perfect symmetry prevents a building from shaping to its surroundings.

On any given site, environmental factors, such as sun, wind, rain, views, noise, and other factors, vary. As architectural form evolves to become more enmeshed with its place, it can take on subtler and subtler geometries. A compelling example is the London City Hall. The early design concept, a transparent torus—sort of a glazed donut—was more purely geometric than the final form, but gradually the architects, Foster + Partners, altered its contours to suit the site. Special digital modeling programs transfigured the rationalized form into one highly responsive to sun, wind, light, and views. The building leans into the sun, shading itself and gathering light onto the riverwalk below. The slender south, east, and west faces minimize solar gain, while the broad north face maximizes views along the Thames. The soft curves diminish wind loads on the surface and structure, as well as air turbulence at the pedestrian level. The form morphs to match its environment, and the result is an astonishing building that requires no mechanical cooling, consumes a quarter of the energy of a typical office building, and uses 75 percent of the surface area of an equivalent rectangular structure.

Instantly, the London City Hall became an icon—ten thousand people visited in the first weekend alone. What draws people to this place? Is it sheer novelty or something deeper? Certainly, curiosity about energy efficiency cannot fully account for the interest, so its power of attraction must be greater than its ability to save power. Believing another kind of power explains its looks, design critic Deyan Sudjic calls the City Hall a piece of political theater, its "comically overblown" ramp corkscrewing a stage-set debate hall that will sit empty most of the time but remain visible to all of London.

Yet, the image of the building arose not out of a misplaced desire for spectacle but out of a careful process of fitting shape to place. In an essay titled "Laws of Form," Hugh Whitehead, director of Foster's digital modeling team, writes that the design called for "radical new solutions to the control of geometry and . . . architectural expression." The word *radical*, he explains, is significant because it literally means "back to roots," and "returning to 'first principles' is the only way to be original." But *original* seems less appropriate than *originary*, creating new foundations that unite the universal laws of physics with the unique circumstances of place. Foster compares the City Hall to a pebble on the shore, its gray surface reflecting river and sky. But, also like water-worn stone, the form is honed by its environs into something essential, elemental, raw but polished. The appeal of this building is how it can become an integral part of its surroundings and still feel so distinctive—a strong hand in a silk glove.

Tradition and Innovation.

Foster + Partners, Masdar City, UAE.

An amalgam of the traditional Middle Eastern walled city and
the most advanced green building innovation. Deep, narrow
corridors in this all-pedestrian community keep the walkways
in shade and channel breezes across fountains. The orientation
keeps out blasts of hot desert wind but gathers cool night breezes.

8 | The Natural Selection of Cities

*The cities of human beings are as natural, being a product
of one form of nature, as are the colonies of prairie dogs or
the beds of oysters.*

—*Jane Jacobs*

In 2006, *An Inconvenient Truth*, Al Gore's Oscar-winning documentary
about global warming, was marketed as "by far the most terrifying film you'll
ever see." The most terrifying for me, however, was another film that same
year: *Idiocracy*, Mike Judge's dark satirical comedy about the dumbing down
of humanity and the world. Five hundred years in the future, everyone is
a moron, and the environment reflects it. Crops are fed with sports drink,

signs are crooked and misspelled, and every available surface is plastered with corporate logos, so entire cities look like NASCAR uniforms. Buildings teeter more than the tower of Pisa, barely held together by guy-wires and duct tape. In the background of this wasteland looms an enormous, neighborhood-sized low-rise that turns out to be a colossal Costco. Big Box retail has become Really Big Box.

If Judge's sardonic vision of the future sounds far-fetched, consider the trends today. Over the past several decades, the public realm increasingly has given in to private commercial interests, and communities have become routinely cheap and generic. In the last quarter of the twentieth century, the United States converted 25 million acres, or 39,000 square miles, of rural land to subdivisions, strip malls, freeways, airports, and other low-density development. According to the U.S. Census, since 1980 the amount of retail space per capita has increased nearly tenfold, from five to fifty, while the number of owners has decreased dramatically. In the 1990s, 5,000 independent hardware stores were displaced by 1,500 Big Boxes owned by two corporations. Five times less efficient with land than their urban equivalents, the largest of those stores are 250,000 square feet, the equivalent of 125 homes—a whole subdivision.

Ecosystems that have enriched the land for centuries, even millennia, are replaced by fast-food franchises that disappear every decade or two, so today's malls become tomorrow's trash. In 2009, Circuit City closed all 567 of its U.S. stores, leaving 18 million square feet of vacant space to languish. When Wal-Mart proposed a new store outside Lake Placid, New York, the city estimated that it would take fourteen years to refill the downtown retail space likely to become "chronically vacant," setting off what city officials called "a net downward spiral in the psychological, visual, and economic character" of the community. Retailers plunk down lifeless, windowless structures outside the city limits and kill the traditional street life downtown. Sprawl breeds blight.

It also damages environmental and human health. Larger footprints mean longer commutes, and the organization Friends of the Earth calculates that just ten miles of a new four-lane highway can create the equivalent lifetime emissions of forty-seven thousand Hummers. The public health implications are equally alarming. A Georgia Tech study shows that every hour per day spent in a car increases the likelihood of obesity by 6 percent, whereas walkable, mixed-use neighborhoods decrease it by 7 percent. The longer your commute, the lower your emotional and physical health, according to a 2010 Gallup poll. In 2011, Swedish researchers found that people who commute more than 45 minutes per day are 40 percent more likely to divorce. The way we shape cities is killing the land, our families, and our communities all at once.

In sustainability's triple bottom line, the environment, society, and economics have equal value, but in the growth of cities, economics far outweighs the other two, and the results can be astonishingly ugly. "Industrialism, the main creative force of the 19th century," wrote the critic Lewis Mumford, "produced the most degraded human environment the world had yet seen." In the middle of the twentieth century, urban theorist Kevin Lynch lamented: "A beautiful and delightful city environment is an oddity, some would say an impossibility. Not one American city larger than a village is of consistently fine quality." At the end of the century, James Howard Kunstler declared in *The Geography of Nowhere*: "80% of everything ever built in America has been built in the last fifty years, and most of it is depressing, brutal, ugly, unhealthy, and spiritually degrading." Architect Ken Yeang has written that "saving the environment from continued devastation by our built environment is the single most important issue for our tomorrow." But the devastation *of* the built environment is just as much at risk.

"Cities are inherently the 'greenest' of all places."

—*Douglas Foy and Robert Healy*

Today, for the first time in history, more people live in urban areas than anywhere else, and the United Nations estimates that by the year 2040, more than 80 percent of the world's population could be city dwellers. During the past two decades, megacities such as Mumbai and Bangalore have doubled in population, and during the next two, according to projections, the United States will need 400 billion square feet of new built space to accommodate conventional growth. Of course, that growth doesn't have to be harmful. Designer Shane Keaney has calculated that if everyone in the United States lived with the density of Brooklyn, we could all fit in an area the size of New Hampshire, the fifth-smallest state. If the area were square, it would measure about a hundred miles wide, and you could ride a bike to the other side of the "country" in a day. Writes Keaney: "We'd all be neighbors."

Plentiful land and cheap oil gave birth to sprawl, but these are things of the past. The challenges of the future require rethinking the design of cities. Embracing greater density, diversity, cleaner fuels, and healthier lifestyles, as well as the subtle natural and cultural variations between one region and another, will help create richer places—a new Geography of Somewhere. We can continue to create "spiritually degrading" environments or, instead, we can choose to craft places of greater grace. The aesthetics of ecology can shape not just products and buildings but whole cities as well.

Size Matters

Picture the most environmentally intelligent city you can imagine. What does it look like? Your mental image might resemble such designer fantasies as Ebenezer Howard's Garden City (1902) or Frank Lloyd Wright's Broadacre City (1932)—sleek towers nestled in lush forests, where a stroll down Main Street feels like a walk in the woods. Or maybe you're thinking of small towns such as Hastings, Nebraska (population twenty-five thousand), which Yahoo! named "the greenest city in America" in 2007. Or you might have in mind something more nostalgic, such as Grover's Corners, the fictional hamlet made famous in Thornton Wilder's *Our Town*, New Urbanism's literary ancestor. Going back at least as far as Jefferson's ideal of an agrarian arcadia, America has carried a romantic torch for rural villages. Idyllic little towns must be the greenest, right?

Actually, small towns are steeped in mythology that doesn't necessarily help the environmental cause. "The old paradigm of the pollution-filled city as a blight on the landscape and the leafy-green suburbs as the ideal is outdated," write Douglas Foy and Robert Healy in the *New York Times*. "Cities, often congested, dense, and enormous consumers of resources, would not be the place one might first turn for environmental solutions. In fact, cities are inherently the 'greenest' of all places." Because they use energy, water, land, and transportation much more effectively than suburbs or small towns do, cities are what Foy and Healy call "the Saudi Arabia of energy efficiency—vast mines of potential energy savings."

> "Cities conform to certain universal dynamics—just like biological organisms."
>
> —*Geoffrey West*

In fact, recent research reveals that the bigger the city, the better. In 2007, a ground-breaking study led by Geoffrey West of the Santa Fe Institute showed that cities conform to the phenomenon known as "biological scaling." All organisms operate in similar ways despite differences in size—metabolically, an elephant is a lot like a mouse, just bigger. A larger mammal has a slower heart rate and therefore a longer life, so the bigger the animal, the more efficiently it uses energy. Cities are the same—the larger they are, the more potentially economical they can be with resources. Analyzing various data, including electrical usage, gas consumption, and lengths of roads, West and his team found that "regardless of size and location, cities conform to certain universal dynamics—just like biological organisms."

In terms of per capita consumption, New York, the largest U.S. city, is significantly more efficient than Hastings. Although the Big Apple didn't make Yahoo!'s list, it is in fact more efficient per person than any other American city. The reason is density—more people per square foot equals lower average waste. Architect James Wines has called the skyscraper "the most anti-ecological of all building types," but in fact apartments in larger multitenant buildings tend to be smaller and more compact than freestanding houses and therefore consume less and conserve more. Size matters. Carbon emissions in New York City are less than a third of the national average, and typical electricity use is 75 percent lower than Dallas. Because walking and public transit are popular, gasoline consumption approximates U.S. levels from the 1920s. "By the most significant measures," writes David Owen in the *New Yorker*, "New York is the greenest community in the United States, and one of the greenest cities in the world." When it comes to energy efficiency, it doesn't take a village—it takes a metropolis.

Identity and Ecology

Nonetheless, the most efficient places are not necessarily the most enjoyable. In *Cities Ranked & Rated*, Bert Sperling and Peter Sander review four hundred cities, and the most "livable," they find, are mostly smaller, diverse, pedestrian-friendly places, such as Charlottesville, Virginia, and Santa Fe, New Mexico (numbers 1 and 2). In the tug-of-war between conservation and comfort, big cities can be more efficient, but smaller towns are more inviting.

Or are they? In *Who's Your City?*, Richard Florida shows that while some cities are better than others, what makes them better has nothing to do with size, for our love of a place is defined more by its character than by its complexity. In *The Image of the City*, his landmark book on urban iconography, Lynch called this character *imageability*, "that quality in a physical object which gives it a high probability of evoking a strong image in any given observer." Recently highlighted by the Robert Wood Johnson Foundation as the first of five strategies to promote healthy living environments,

imageability can be created by the quality of a city's architecture, the shape of streetscapes, the interaction with the terrain, the choreography of vistas, and the character of transit and infrastructure, such as Paris's sinewy Metro stops, San Francisco's quaint cable cars, or London's bright red phone booths and double-decker buses, all memorable icons of place.

Lynch lists three aspects of a city's image: *identity*, its individuality and distinction from other things; *structure*, the physical relationship between buildings and other structures; and *meaning*, "whether practical or emotional." In a telling passage, Lynch chooses to focus on the first two while avoiding the third altogether: "So various are the individual meanings of a city, even while its form may be easily communicable, that it appears possible to separate meaning from form."

To see meaning and form as separable exposes a bias that defeats the purpose of sustainable communities. Settled cultures, indigenous and ancient peoples, have understood the world only in relation to natural context, and a community that has thrived in harmony with its environment for many, many generations sees form and meaning as integral to place. Anthropologist Keith

Basso describes the Apache worldview: "Placeless events are an impossibility, everything that happens must happen somewhere. The location of an event is an integral aspect of the event itself, and therefore indentifying the event's location is essential to properly depicting—and effectively picturing—the event's occurrence."

By contrast, modern urban theory often ignores or dismisses natural setting entirely. Lynch suggests that adapting to the natural is antiquated and unsophisticated: "Primitive man was forced to improve his environmental image by adapting his perception to the given landscape. He could [only] effect minor changes in his environment. . . . Only powerful civilizations can begin to act on their total environment at a significant scale. The conscious remolding of the large-scale physical environment has been possible only recently, and so the problem of environmental imageability is a new one." The "primitive" perception of the environment necessarily adapted to a given place, whereas industrial civilization, unfettered by such constraints, can "remold" the environment to fit purely human motives. An industrialized design sensibility separates space from place and form from

Regional Echoes.

Michael Sorkin Studio, Penang Peaks, Penang, Malaysia.

The new development of exotic spiral towers draws inspiration from various regional influences, such as local arcade shops and Southeast Asia's towering coastal mountains.

meaning, but naturalized communities consider such divisions preposterous. Lynch bemoans inconsistent impressions of places, but he underestimates the importance of natural context, the one thing sure to create collective meaning.

The public images and local cultures of the most memorable places grew out of their ancient settings. Los Angeles sits between ocean and mountain; Denver, between mountain and plain. Try to imagine San Francisco without thinking of steep hills, the Bay, the Golden Gate, or looming fog. Picture Seattle without mountains, the Sound, or the constant drizzle of rain. Imagine Chicago without its lake, or Miami without its beaches. If a city is as natural as a prairie dog colony, as Jane Jacobs suggested, splitting up form, meaning, and context is like trying to build the colony without the prairie. A strong, clear identity isn't enough, for the image of the ecological city must be relevant and responsive to its natural setting.

The Setting of the City

Every city everywhere is to some degree shaped by its setting, however subtly or substantially. Every place reveals a relationship between natural conditions and human motives, and what matters most is whether that relationship is a contest or a collaboration, whether nature and city are adversary or ally. The distinction between the natural and the unnatural is less relevant than the degree to which nature influences a city's form and performance. How intricately woven is a city in its surroundings? How well does its shape suit its place?

Take New York. Manhattan's grid plan often is described as a relentlessly artificial imposition on the land; in *Delirious New York*, architect Rem Koolhaas claims the city is intended "to exist in a world totally fabricated by man." The original Commissioners' Plan of 1811 supposedly was suggested by laying wire mesh over a map of Manhattan. Yet, the most identifiable aspect of the city, its verticality, came about primarily because the narrowness of the island created space limitations—if you can't grow outward, grow upward. The modern skyscraper sprang from the fact that twenty thousand years ago two rivers eroded a piece of land twelve miles long but only two miles wide.

The plan of Manhattan is smarter than conventional wisdom concedes. Not a square grid, most of the streets run river to river instead of uptown and down, partly because the planners assumed that maritime commerce along the riverfronts would create more crosstown traffic. The blocks are nearly five times longer in the east–west dimension (avenue to avenue) than in the north–south (street to street), so most buildings avoid the low morning and afternoon sun, ensuring plenty of light without too much heat. Because the grid sits at a twenty-nine-degree angle off of true north, potentially every building on every street can receive direct daylight every day of the year. In 1916, the plan gained vertical expression after zoning laws requiring setbacks to bring more light to the streets produced an iconic skyline of sculpted towers, such as the Chrysler Building. This "world totally fabricated by man" is actually a world partly shaped by the sun.

On the other hand, most of the island was formed through massive cutting and filling to reform its natural contours, and Central Park, the beautiful lungs of New York, is drained marshland. The name *Manhattan* originally came from an Algonquin word for "island of hills," but little is left of them. In 1818, when the Chelsea property of Clement Clark Moore, famed author of "A Visit from St. Nicholas," was split in two by Ninth Avenue, he wrote: "Nothing is to be left unmolested which does not coincide with the street commissioner's plummet and level." The planners, he complained, "would have cut down the seven hills of Rome, on which are erected her triumphant monuments of beauty and magnificence, and have thrown them into the Tyber or the Pomptine marshes."

Nevertheless, traces of the original terrain still shape the character of the city. Along the island's major natural ridgeline, an ancient deer and mountain lion route, Lenape natives carved the Wickquasgeck Trail, which Dutch settlers later called *Breede weg* and the English renamed Broadway. Running due north and south, the boulevard angles across the grain of the grid, leaving irregular plots at many intersections, and these form the most famous public spaces, such as Times Square, where Broadway crosses Seventh Avenue and 42nd Street. The shapes and images of New York's most recognizable places evolved directly out of a natural source, a prehistoric wildlife trail.

The Natural City

Manhattan's example highlights how nature can subtly affect the form and identity of a city. An urgent priority for planners is to provide context and meaning for a community by enriching the connections between the natural and cultural environments. Hailed as the world's first carbon-neutral, zero-waste city, Masdar City is a six-square-kilometer development outside Abu Dhabi, in the United Arab Emirates. While its buildings individually are required to surpass existing standards of environmental performance, the real story is the urban plan. Combining the ancient principles of a Middle Eastern walled city and the latest advances in green technology, Masdar draws from the best intelligence of tradition and innovation. Solar and wind farms outside the walls provide clean energy while freeing up the internal layout to be developed around what works for people, not power.

A city without cars, Masdar is a pedestrian haven, no point being more than two hundred meters from public transit and services. A compact network of narrow streets and shaded walkways protects residents from heat and glare while creating humanely scaled public spaces. The orientation of the plan shields the interior of the city from blasts of hot desert wind but gathers cool night breezes. Masdar aims to create not just an energy-efficient development but also a world-class city with an excellent quality of life. The developers declare that it will "redefine the design and construction of cities in the future," but the most successful thing about Masdar is how it unites ancient and modern, past and future.

As they evolve more sensitively, cities could become more and more like natural habitats, seemingly inevitable manifestations of elemental forces. In this event, cities would be not only natural, in the sense that Jane Jacobs describes, but also naturally selected, in a Darwinian sense. In evolutionary biology, natural selection refers to variations in form that create a survival advantage, one wholly contingent on an organism's surroundings, including climate, terrain, and resources. As with biological form, naturally selected urban form is better fit to its environment. That cities don't all look the same makes them more identifiable but also more resilient, better adapted to their individual climates and contexts.

Natural selection applies to both the internal and external structure of a city. In his brilliant essay "A City Is Not a Tree," Christopher Alexander distinguishes between a *natural city* and an *artificial city*: "It is more and more

"Planning" from the Bottom Up.
Aranda/Lasch, "Rules of Six."
An experiment in self-assembly, the study applies algorithms mimicking natural patterns to six-sided forms of varying sizes, the hexagon being an incredibly efficient and durable structure found in honeycombs and geological formations. The result suggests an urban-scale landscape that is grown more than planned.

widely recognized today that there is some essential ingredient missing from artificial cities. When compared with ancient cities that have acquired the patina of life, our modern attempts to create cities artificially are, from a human point of view, entirely unsuccessful." One missing ingredient, says Alexander, is complexity. In an artificial city, form is imposed from the top down, as a simple hierarchy of relationships (a "tree"), while the natural city evolves from the bottom up as an interwoven network of relationships Alexander calls a semi-lattice. Whenever a city is "thought out" instead of "grown," it is bound to get a treelike structure, an overly simplified footprint. A natural city tends to have a subtler structure but also an equally complex underlying set of relationships. This is the geometry of ecology.

As urban plans begin to mimic natural systems, they take on a geometry known as a "scale-free network." Any self-organizing community—from an ecosystem to the Internet—tends to evolve around complex but predictable traits that appear haphazard but actually have an inherent logic, not perfectly regular but not completely random either. Stronger intersections evolve around highly trafficked places—on the Internet, it would be sites such as Google or Yahoo!, and in a city it might be the market square or city hall.

Because these hubs strengthen the connectivity and resiliency of the overall plan, the geometry is known also as a "small-world network."

So far, the theory behind such networks has focused mostly on abstract or intangible systems, such as social circles, but in actuality the science originated when solving an urban planning puzzle—the most efficient path for traversing the seven bridges of Königsberg, Germany. That was three hundred years ago. In recent years, Frei Otto and others have experimented with patterns that optimize the lengths of pathways within a city plan, generating intricate but highly efficient shapes whose fractal nature has been shown to have wide aesthetic appeal. These irregular urban plans, adapted to terrain, could be the hallmarks of a more "natural" city form.

From the Ground Up

Whereas Lynch calls the modern city a "conscious remolding of the large-scale physical environment," settled cultures instead mold themselves to suit their environment. Industrial civilization moves mountains and levels land to make way for cookie-cutter communities, but the natural city honors the special character of the present ground. One is generic and placeless; the other, idiosyncratic and unique. Too many American cities conform to Gertrude Stein's quip about Oakland that "there's no *there* there." Living communities create more *here* here.

Many of the world's most memorable places draw their character from topography. Nestled into a south-facing hollow under the enormous outcropping of a canyon wall near Four Corners in Colorado, the Anasazi cliff dwelling of Mesa Verde withdraws from the high summer sun but bathes in the low winter light. In the handful of fishing villages making up the *Cinque Terre* ("five lands") on the Italian Riviera, the houses cling to the shady face of a deep gorge, protected from harsh storm winds while the ravine coaxes salt-licked air up from the shoreline.

Working with the land, not against it, can ensure incredible longevity. Taking advantage of natural slopes and water sources, Chinese rice terraces have been active for five thousand years or more. Natural springs spill downhill through the irrigation channels of the Philippines' Banaue Rice Terraces, which have been continually used for two millennia. The entire culture of the Inca evolved around the impossibly steep slopes of the Andes

Mountains. At altitudes of up to fourteen thousand feet with slopes of sixty-five degrees or more, Peruvian peoples have flourished as vertical communities. Their dramatically terraced highways—easily traversed by sure-footed llamas but terrifying to the horses of Spanish conquistadors—were so beautifully crafted to the setting that some have lasted half a millennium without any maintenance.

If there is one city that is a living testament to both the beauty and tragedy of terrain, it is New Orleans. The fan-shaped street grid follows the Mississippi as it snakes through the Crescent City, so the form and experience of the plan entirely defer to the river. The parallel streets continually shift at the break lines, so at eye level the urban fabric appears perpetually in motion, an urban scenography generated directly by the shape of the land. As in many places, topography determined both the history and demographics of New Orleans. The earliest settlements, beginning with the French Quarter in 1789, took to the high ground at the river bend, and as the city expanded and pressure for space grew, more and more people—typically lower-income populations—spilled into the lower areas. By the time Hurricane Katrina hit in 2005, the wealthy were safely ensconced above while the poor lingered below. After the deluge devastated the flood zone, it became all too easy to criticize the city's growth by suggesting that the lowlands should never have been occupied and shouldn't be redeveloped, but this attitude sees both the topographical and socioeconomic complexion of the city too narrowly.

New Orleans is and always has been a city of the water, but over the last century it seems to have forgotten itself. Hubris led to an infrastructure based on sheer force, with thicker and thicker walls and barriers trying to hold back the sea. But rethinking the very nature of coastal cities is inevitable now. Some post-Katrina proposals suggest letting the lowlands become occupied lagoons, with housing hovering above the tidal basin. Stilt villages have thrived forever in the Gulf of Thailand, so why not the Gulf of Mexico? Using a minimum elevation that is safely above the floodplain, new construction in New Orleans is beginning to establish an invisible line several feet above the ground, a kind of imaginary terrain above sea level. *Aqua firma.*

In the wake of Katrina, a consortium of New Orleans architects, planners, engineers, and policy makers worked closely with counterparts from Amsterdam and Rotterdam to share knowledge and strategies among delta communities with very similar challenges but separated by five thousand miles. Inspired by the Netherlands' "Living with Water" development policies, the

Ebb and Flow.

De Urbanisten, Water Squares, Rotterdam.
Rills and runnels prevent flooding by introducing water thoroughly into the fabric of the city. During a storm, water would activate landscapes and public plazas as social amenities, transforming a potential threat into a thing of delight.

(a) Regular rain (up to 5mm, frequent)
(b) Temperate rain (6mm, 20 to 50 times per year)
(c) Heavy rain (11 mm, 4 to 11 times per year)

"Dutch Dialogues" propose a subtle integration of water and land. Instead of ramparts attempting to keep the water out entirely, a series of rills and runnels would introduce water into the fabric of the city without displacing any housing or other development. A single line of defense against an enormous volume of water would be replaced by spreading smaller amounts throughout the entire community. The designers call the system "vascular," rather than muscular. During a rainstorm, water would activate landscapes and public plazas as social amenities, transforming a potential threat into a thing of delight.

Water, Water, Everywhere

How cities will adapt to changing water conditions has become a critical question in the face of global warming, since some 90 percent of the world's largest cities are located on waterfronts. In the past century, the earth's surface temperature has risen nearly two degrees Fahrenheit, and another four degrees could dramatically alter the planet through extreme storms, flooding, and rising sea levels. Hotter oceans have expanded—up to eight inches in height already—and melting glaciers in Greenland and Antarctica continue to pump up the volume. The flow of ice into the sea has doubled over the past decade and over the next century could cause a twenty-foot rise, making densely populated regions like the Nile Delta uninhabitable. In the United States, even three more feet would flood every city on the eastern seaboard. Whole coastlines would retreat as water spills inland and redraws the map of the world.

Among the ten places most threatened by future flooding, according to the Organisation for Economic Co-operation and Development (OECD), is New York City, and some designers are already planning ahead. In their winning entry to the History Channel's first City of the Future competition (2006), Architecture Research Office (ARO) imagined a postdiluvian Big Apple as Big Venice—canals for streets and boats in lieu of cars. To maintain comparable density after the flood, ARO would insert new buildings over the public right-of-way. Spanning curb to curb, these unique structures, called "vanes," would become reeflike foundations for a new communal habitat. "We have nature all around us—it's the *water*," says ARO's Adam Yarinsky. "It's not green space, but it's natural." Rediscovering the city's relationship with the rivers, he feels, can "transform a catastrophe into a revelation."

Three years later, Yarinsky and others proposed a more ambitious and comprehensive plan for New York Harbor. Instead of trying to hold back a storm by building a single, massive structure like New Orleans's failed levees, the group designed a "soft infrastructure" of landscapes sprinkled throughout the Upper Bay. Boomerang-shaped barrier islands establish a gradient between Lower Manhattan and possible storm surges from the south. Inspired by oyster beds—and therefore making Jane Jacobs's analogy literal—the islands are shaped and arranged to slow down and diffuse the waves. Over time, the structures would accumulate sediment and grow naturally into earthen mounds. Constructed wetlands and artificial islands would create wildlife habitat, and a network of parks and recreational spaces would offer new social space, so the proposal would turn defensive infrastructure into natural and cultural services. "Building barriers is not enough," Nordenson says. "We can accommodate climate change through the creation of new urban space."

> "We can accommodate climate change through the creation of new urban space."
> *—Guy Nordenson*

The design firm Field Operations pictures a similarly hopeful future in Biopolis, their sketch portrait of Lower Manhattan's projected history from 1660 to 2200. As landscape architect James Corner explains, the first four centuries of the city's development have been driven by economics—the landfill that produced the World Trade Center site, for instance, maximized available real estate while severing the traditional interplay between river and land by filling in the old slips and wharfs. But Corner sees the city shifting from economics to ecology, becoming an integrated habitat of people, fauna, and flora—what he calls "a biological engine" and "an incubator for new life." Instead of containing landscape within clearly defined boundaries—the Central Park model—vegetation would become the backbone of the community's development. To accommodate higher sea levels, the southern tip ultimately would become a detached island, which Corner dubs "micro-Manhattan." A ring beach at the edge would give residents direct access to the water. "Too often development and sustainability are seen as opposed," says Corner. "But the two should go hand-in-hand. A dense urban complex can be part of an ecological landscape." Biopolis prepares for a future in which water will commingle with life in the city.

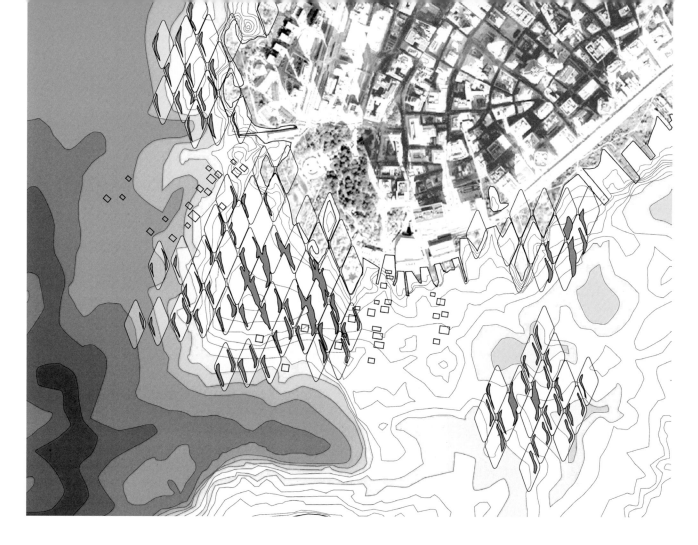

Cities Gone Wild

Biopolis represents an emerging vision of the built environment that Corner and others call "landscape urbanism." Its practice rejects the split between town and country by recognizing that cities are ecosystems where cultural and natural forms mix. Biopolis transforms natural materials, air, light, water, and energy into what Corner calls "radically new amalgams of nature and urban life." The city becomes a habitat explicitly conceived for all life, human and otherwise. Richard Louv, who coined the term *nature-deficit disorder*, considers such countrified urbanism a vital strategy for immersing children in the natural world. "Cities gone wild," he calls it.

   Conceiving the city as possibly more landscape than streetscape is a compelling reversal, and the advantages of abundant planting are well established.

City like an Oyster Bed.

Guy Nordenson Associates, Catherine Seavitt Studio, and Architecture Research Office, Palisade Bay, New York Harbor. A "soft infrastructure" of boomerang-shaped barrier islands slows and diffuses storm surges, accumulating sediment over time and growing naturally into earthen wetlands, wildlife habitat, and community parks.

The Birth of the Agropolis.
Terreform, New York City (Steady) State.
This proposal envisions the city as a
closed-loop system that uses only local
food and resources, and virtually every
surface becomes a productive landscape.
Vertical farming towers stand in
the background.

Urban forestry produces oxygen, absorbs carbon, provides shade, buffers wind, softens noise, protects paving, regulates temperature, and lowers energy consumption. The evaporation from a single large tree can produce the cooling effect of ten room-sized air conditioners operating around the clock. The sociological benefits are equally dramatic. Views and access to living landscapes improve productivity in offices, test scores in schools, patient recovery in hospitals, social interaction in neighborhoods, crime rates in communities, and even harmony in the home, since greenery has been linked to less domestic violence.

According to the Landscape and Human Health Laboratory at the University of Illinois, lushly vegetated neighborhoods report 80 percent fewer

aggressive disturbances. In a study conducted at a Chicago public housing development, residents of buildings with more trees said that they knew their neighbors better, socialized with them more often, had stronger feelings of community, and felt safer and better adjusted than did residents of barren but otherwise identical buildings. Landscape urbanism makes cities cleaner, quieter, safer, stronger, healthier, more economical, efficient, comfortable, peaceful, and beautiful.

Urban ecology can create environments that are not just ornamental and recreational but also productive—by reconnecting where people live with what they eat. Urban agriculture is gaining ground, for good reason. Compared to industrially produced food shipped from afar, locally grown produce tastes fresher, supports the municipal economy, and saves huge amounts of energy, emissions, waste, transportation, and infrastructure maintenance. A produce garden also is a much more efficient use of land than is the token park or lawn. According to Michael Hough, in *Cities and Natural Process*, the rate of energy to maintain 6.5 million hectares of residential lawns in the United States significantly exceeds the rate for commercial cornfields in the equivalent amount of soil. Comparing a typical grass lawn to an alfalfa patch of the same size, Hough shows that the lawn needs three times the amount of energy in maintenance but yields less energy and zero crops or food.

Urban agriculture is smart and elegant, but soon it also may be inevitable. Columbia University biologist Dickson Despommier estimates that to feed the expected population in 2050, we'll need about 2.1 billion acres of new land—roughly the size of Brazil. Yet, today, more than 80 percent of arable land is already in use. If current farming practices continue, in a few decades there simply won't be enough land to feed everyone. Despommier's solution? Vertical farming. He proposes transferring new food production from sprawling rural farms to environmentally controlled multistory buildings in urban centers—cornfields in the sky. These hothouse towers would dramatically condense the footprint of land required while also improving quality and yield and nearly eliminating transport-related waste and energy consumption—by growing food right where it's needed. Vertical farming would give birth to a new building type, the garden high-rise, populating a new kind of community, the agropolis. The community that feeds itself would be visible in its skyline. The image of the city would testify not to wealth but to health, growing an urban iconography that mixes sustainability and sustenance.

Cities of Tomorrow

Inner-city gardens in lower-income communities have been demonstrating the beautiful union of economy and ecology for generations. Economically disadvantaged peoples often show the greatest ingenuity. Necessity is the mother of invention, and sustainability is born from need—"doing more with less," in Buckminster Fuller's words. If innovation rises out of a crisis, conditions today are ripe for design revolution. The United Nations calculates that over a billion people, one sixth of humanity and a third of all city dwellers, live in slums, virtually all of them in the developing regions of Asia, Africa, and South America. A 2007 *Economist* report on Dharavi, a Mumbai slum, estimated "maybe a million residents crammed into a square mile of low-rise wood, concrete and rusted iron."

Already thick with people, impoverished urban areas are expected to double in population over the next two decades. Planning cannot keep up, so an increasingly large number of people fend for themselves, ad-libbing their own housing, often illegally, in whatever space they can find at the edges of existing communities, usually on slopes deemed unbuildable. From the discarded scraps and shards of their neighbors, they scrape together lean-tos and shanties to fashion a community of their own—do-it-yourself cities. As the growth of developing urban regions far outpaces that of developed countries, improvised communities are multiplying and, according to the United Nations, "quickly becoming the visual expression of urban poverty."

Nearly a third of São Paulo and a fifth of Rio de Janeiro inhabitants live in squatter villages, or *favelas*. The Portuguese word originated with the first such shantytown, cobbled together in 1897 on the hillside of Rio's Morro da Providência by twenty thousand landless veterans returning from the Canudos Civil War. They renamed the hill Morro da Favela, after the hardy plant (*faveleira resistente*) that thrived on the battlefield site of a key victory during the war. Eventually, the favela became a refuge for freed black slaves, and a pattern emerged that is unique among impoverished urban communities. Because its very existence is unsanctioned, governments do not recognize a favela as an official community, socially or physically, so its inhabitants are not just poor, they are displaced, dispossessed, exiled.

In *Shadow Cities,* his intimate portrait of squatter communities, journalist Robert Neuwirth describes their essential paradox: while they lack what we might consider the basic necessities of a city, their quality of life can be deeply fulfilling. Recounting his time living in favelas on four continents,

Neuwirth tells the story of Armstrong O'Brian, who shared a tiny corrugated-metal hut with three other men in Southland, a shantytown on the edge of Nairobi, Kenya. There was no running water, no toilet, and no sewers or sanitation, and their electricity, illegally tapped, powered only a single light-bulb. Yet, according to Neuwirth, O'Brian "treasured the quality of life in his neighborhood. . . . Southland wasn't constrained by its material conditions. Instead, the human spirit radiated out from the metal walls and garbage heaps to offer something no legal neighborhood could: freedom." The squatters don't own their land, but they hold it close nonetheless, and the solidarity within these communities can be powerful. "This place is very addictive," O'Brian told Neuwirth. "Once you have stayed here, you cannot go back."

How can it be that places of such apparent squalor, assembled haphazardly from discards and debris, can be so captivating? Favela dwellers, or *favelados*, have no official "rights" as such, and their communities aren't recognized by any legal authority and often don't even appear on maps—invisible cities. But their nonconformity may actually explain their power, which

"Slums of Hope."

Favela, Rio de Janeiro.

The fastest-growing settlements today, squatter communities often lack clean infrastructure but show many of the traits of sustainable development—compact footprint, high density, low-impact or zero grading, low energy use, reclaimed materials, humane scale, variety, affordability, vibrant social interaction, and a tangible sense of community. "Once you have stayed here, you cannot go back."

springs from self-determination, not official sanction. Though their roots are shallow, favelas are, like the plant from which they get their name, tough survivors. And like any ecosystem, they adapt, they evolve, they endure—what works lives; what doesn't dies. Bureaucracy-free, they are nimbler than conventional municipalities; lacking any order or plan imposed from the outside, they are completely self-generating and consequently can have a more natural sense of community than many planned cities.

"The favela is a community. I feel I am cared for and the people care about me," writes DJ Zezinho, an activist born and raised in Rocinha, Brazil's largest favela. "Outside the favela people only care about money and material items, not people." After living in the United States for a while, he returned to Rocinha and started a nonprofit organization to promote education and awareness about squatter communities. "I believe that the lack of empathy and understanding from outsiders remains a big obstacle to long-term improvement of life in the favelas." Living in what he calls the *asfalto* world of conventional cities, those outsiders assume Zezinho's world should be wiped clean.

Neuwirth insists that tearing down and rebuilding squatter villages will only further displace their residents by producing unaffordable housing. "The true challenge," he writes, "is not to eradicate these communities but to stop treating them as slums—that is, as horrific, scary and criminal—and start treating them as neighborhoods that can be improved." The fastest-growing settlements today, squatter communities are quickly becoming the norm. As Neuwirth explains: "Squatters mix more concrete than any developer. They lay more brick than any government. They have created a huge hidden economy. . . . [They] are the largest builders of housing in the world—and they are creating the cities of tomorrow." Like a sapling wood emerging at the edge of an ancient forest, the favela could be the first sign of a new kind of city, the future of urbanism.

> Favelas could be the first sign of a new kind of city, the future of urbanism.

World-class cities such as New York and London, Neuwirth points out, began with squatter-style neighborhoods and didn't have paved roads, electricity, or sanitation systems until relatively late in their histories. In Rocinha, we find not a temporary nuisance but a nascent community, the seeds of a someday Paris or Barcelona. Favelas are starter cities. In fact, they already show many of the earmarks associated with sustainable development: compact footprint, high density, low-impact grading, low energy use, reclaimed materials, humane scale, variety, affordability, vibrant social interaction, and a tangible sense of community.

Nikos Salingaros, author of *Principles of Urban Structure*, believes favelas show more promise for longevity than do many planned communities because they begin not at the grand scale of cartographers but at the intimate scale of the inhabitants. The basic building blocks of the favela are not district and artery—they are body and dwelling. The informal building patterns emerge not from abstract theories about order but from human intuition for creating habitat. Many of their forms and spaces have been shown to exhibit the geometry of natural fractals. This is instinctive urbanism. Like an Italian hill town, a favela's shapes and textures can be irresistible.

The future of cities could lie not in the designer dreams of a Masdar or a Biopolis but, instead, in these least glamorous of places. Will the next generation of living community be some hybrid of metropolis and favela, combining the health, safety, and stable infrastructure of the one with the flexibility, resourcefulness, and communal creativity of the other? Spontaneous settlements create new visions that question customary understandings of community, property, urbanism, waste, value, and even beauty. Rocinha has built a vibrant community and compelling urbanism out of found land and found materials, the discarded debris of the *asfalto* city. Carving homes out of garbage dumps, favelas are monuments to ingenuity and endurance. These "slums of hope," as the United Nations has called them, could be the communities of the future.

One World.

"Blue Marble," from Apollo 17, December 1972.

The most reproduced image in history, it changed how we see the earth and one another, and it helped launch the sustainability movement. The true impact of the space program came not from its technology but from its imagery.

9 | Visions of Earth

The world is as you see it.

—Hindu Scripture

ON CHRISTMAS EVE 1968, Bill Anders looked out his window and saw something no one had ever seen before. Against a pitch-black sky, framed by a bone-dead, mottled-gray landscape, hovered a hazy half-dome of swirling white and brilliant blue, the only bit of color anywhere in sight. It was a stark scene, a solitary figure floating in "a vast lonely expanse of nothing," as one of his two companions described it, yet it overwhelmed them all with emotion, a kind of awe perhaps previously unfelt by anyone in history. "It was the most beautiful, heart-catching sight of my life," one later recalled. Anders did what every sightseer does—he took a photograph. That quick snapshot became, in the words of biophysicist John Platt, "one of the most powerful images in the minds of men today."

The crew of *Apollo 8*—Anders, Frank Borman, and Jim Lovell—not only were the first people ever to leave orbit and the first to see the dark side of the moon but also were the first to witness Earth intact, not as a fragmentary arc of horizon but as a complete being, an entire world. "We came all this way to the Moon," Anders later recalled, "and yet the most significant thing we're seeing is our own home planet." After the Apollo program ended, the writer Norman Cousins told Congress that the most dramatic event of the lunar voyages "was not that men set foot on the Moon, but that they set eye on the Earth." Michael Collins agreed; though he was there when Neil Armstrong stepped out onto the Sea of Tranquility in 1969, he considered the earlier image "more awe-inspiring than landing on the moon." He called it, simply, "magic."

> "Representations of the globe have exercised an especially powerful grasp on the western imagination."
>
> —*Denis Cosgrove*

Anders's shot, *Earthrise*, has been dubbed "the most influential environmental photograph ever taken," and *Life* magazine lists it as one of "100 Photographs That Changed the World." And yet, almost exactly four years later, Jack Schmitt trumped it. During the last of the Apollo missions, the sixth and final lunar landing, and still the most recent manned flight beyond low orbit, Schmitt captured Earth completely round, unmarred by the moon's shadow. The famous *Blue Marble* photo has become the single most widely reproduced image in history.

These pictures did more than just show us what our planet looks like; they changed how humanity sees itself. The intricate relationships between imagery and ecology, the core subject of this book, begin with visions of the earth itself, for how we see the world affects everything we shape within that world. "Representations of the globe," writes Denis Cosgrove in *Apollo's Eye*, "have exercised an especially powerful grasp on the western imagination." For millennia, those representations were inevitably piecemeal and speculative until Anders's trio gazed through their glass and turned fantasy into reality. Two decades earlier, astronomer Fred Hoyle had predicted that "once a photograph of the Earth, taken from the outside, is available, we shall, in an emotional sense, acquire an additional dimension . . . and a new idea as powerful as any in history will be let loose." The idea behind the image was that we share one world.

"We saw the Earth the size of a quarter," remembers Borman, "and we recognized then that there really is one world." From afar, the planet appeared both beautiful and small, and, suddenly, age-old distinctions of political borders, national territories, and legal property became invisible, insignificant, irrelevant. Seeing this for the first time, many hoped, would stamp out parochial rivalries and kickstart an era of international idealism. A "world outlook," felt science-fiction writer Arthur C. Clarke, might overcome ancient competitions for bits and pieces of land: "It is not easy to see how the more extreme forms of nationalism can long survive when men have seen the Earth in its true perspective as a single small globe against the stars."

A new consciousness really did spring from this new vision. The philosopher William Irwin Thompson called it "a new stage in human culture . . . a planetary society." Its biggest beneficiary was the planet itself, for the four years between *Earthrise* and *Blue Marble* coincided exactly with the birth of what we now call the sustainability movement. In the previous eighty years, new environmental groups had appeared about once a decade; between 1968 and 1972, seven major national organizations came into being. In the middle, in April 1970, was the inaugural Earth Day.

Before that day, the word *ecology* was barely familiar, but that year it filled eighty-six columns in the *New York Times*. Peace activist John McConnell had contemplated the idea of Earth Day a few years earlier, but nothing came of it until the first photo of Earth appeared in *Life* magazine in 1969. Seeing it, he "experienced in a deep and emotional way a new awareness of our planet." This new view of the world encouraged a new worldview: "The Earth as seen from space was the best possible symbol for this purpose." Anders had supplied the environmental cause with its most powerful icon.

The same year that *Blue Marble* appeared saw the publication of *Limits to Growth* (1972), which mathematically proved what the photograph implied—that it's a small world after all. (Not coincidentally, Schmitt's photo appears on the cover of the thirtieth-anniversary edition.) The book also was possibly the first to use the word *sustainability* with its current connotations, and fifteen years later the image of Earth directly influenced how we now define the concept.

In 1987, the United Nations–sponsored study *Our Common Future* began with an overview, "From One Earth to One World": "In the middle of the 20th century, we saw our planet from space for the first time. Historians may eventually find that this vision had a greater impact on thought than did the Copernican revolution of the sixteenth century, which upset the human self-image by revealing that the Earth is not the center of the universe. From space, we see a small and fragile ball dominated not by human activity and edifice but by a pattern of clouds, oceans, greenery, and soils. Humanity's

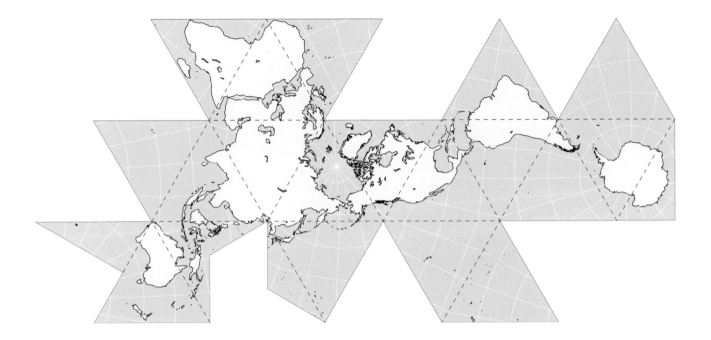

This Island Earth.
Buckminster Fuller,
Dymaxion Projection Map, 1954.
The layout accurately depicted—for
the first time—the entire Earth on a flat
plane, with only the tiniest bit of distortion.
It also broke down barriers between
East and West, North and South, Old and
New, Rich and Poor.

inability to fit its doings into that pattern is changing planetary systems fundamentally. . . . This new reality, from which there is no escape, must be recognized—and managed."

The space race gave us powerful new tools, including many of today's most visible green technologies, such as photovoltaics; yet, the most dramatic impact of the space program lay not in its machinery but in its imagery. "We had a lot of illusions about Earth," recalls futurist Stewart Brand, founder of the *Whole Earth Catalog,* whose cover featured *Earthrise.* "One of them was that it was basically flat and infinite with no finitude to our resources. And we had very stereotyped ideas of what the Earth looked like from space. If you look at all of the images that people made before we had photographs, almost none of them have clouds or weather and climate." In 1966, Brand began distributing buttons with a simple but urgent question: "Why haven't we seen a photograph of the whole Earth yet?" Thousands of these buttons reached policy makers, journalists, activists, and astronauts. "There is such a thing as icons," Brand says, "and icons help frame people's thinking."

From the outset, the conservation movement had been propelled by imagery. In 1837, the French painters of the Barbizon School successfully convinced authorities not to cut down the most picturesque portions of the Fontainebleau Forest, purely for aesthetic reasons. In the United States, Albert Bierstadt's sublime paintings, Ansel Adams's haunting photographs, and others' portraits of the western frontier fueled interest in preserving the natural glories of the American continent. Yet, the image of the planet as a whole shifted the focus from the conservation of wilderness to the preservation of the total environment, including humanity.

Six years before *Earthrise*, Rachel Carson's *Silent Spring* (1962) sounded both a wake-up call about environmental toxicity and a battle cry for ecological health. While Carson was turning her focus inward, to soils and streams, John F. Kennedy was looking outward, delivering his famous speeches to rally Americans to space. Once we got there and looked back, causes once considered separate—wildlife protection, public health, social equity, civil rights, and peace—all came together under the single banner of Earth. This was the dawn of the sustainability movement.

One World

Earlier in the century, Buckminster Fuller had attempted to represent a more inclusive worldview with his Dymaxion Map. An inherent challenge with any atlas is translating the curved faces of Earth onto a flat surface, which distorts the sizes and shapes of land masses. The Mercator Projection, devised by Flemish cartographer Gerardus Mercator in 1569 and still the most common map today, extends the continental lines from a sphere onto a cylinder, dramatically shrinking the top and bottom of the globe. And the point of view—with the equator and the prime meridian at center—reinforces dichotomies between East and West, North and South, Old and New, Rich and Poor. It's a Eurocentric worldview.

Fuller's map, published in 1954, was different in two fundamental ways. First, the geometric layout, composed of icosahedrons, also the basis for his famed geodesic domes, accurately depicted—for the first time—the entire Earth on a flat plane, with only the tiniest bit of distortion, mostly in the oceans. Second, the point of view, from the North Pole, showed the continents as if they are one continuous landmass, what Fuller called "One World Island." If school kids everywhere used such a map to learn geography, how might their understanding of the world change?

Fuller's map anticipated a post-Apollo mindset, which sees Earth not just as an organic whole but as an actual organism. "Viewed from the distance of the Moon, the astonishing thing about the Earth, catching the breath, is that it is alive," announced biologist Lewis Thomas, who felt that life's uniformity is more dramatic than its diversity. "The outstanding spin-off from space research is not new technology," wrote biologist James Lovelock.

"The photographs of the Earth from space were a different kind of mirror than we had ever looked in before."

—*Stewart Brand*

"The real bonus has been that for the first time we have had a chance to look at the Earth from space, and the information gained from seeing from the outside our azure planet in all its global beauty has given rise to a whole new set of questions and answers." Lovelock answered those questions with the Gaia hypothesis, which proposes that life did not simply adapt to the environment—seen on the planetary scale, it also adapted the environment to itself. "Just as the shell is part of the snail," he writes, "so the rocks, the air and the oceans are part of Gaia." New views of Earth created new visions of Earth not just as the setting for living things but also as a living thing itself.

Yet, seen from a distance, Earth didn't just look intact—it also looked small. "Suddenly I knew what a tiny, fragile thing Earth is," remarked Michael Collins, and virtually every Apollo astronaut commented on how they could blot out the entire planet with one thumb. In 1990, when the space probe *Voyager* sent back a photo of Earth from 4 billion miles out, astronomer Carl Sagan called it the "pale blue dot": "Everyone you know, everyone you ever heard of, every human being that ever was, lived out their lives . . . on a mote of dust suspended in a sunbeam." Sagan meant to portray his reverent awe at the enormity of the universe; yet, to describe the entire planet as a "mote of dust," a speck of space detritus, makes it seem both easier to control and easier to devalue—a thing visually and virtually under your thumb.

From the outside, the planet appears as an object, less a home than something we merely occupy. "The photographs of the Earth from space were a different kind of mirror than we had ever looked in before," explains Stewart Brand. "It flips you from the world that we are *in*, to a planet that we are *on*." After *Earthrise*, the *Houston Chronicle* declared that space travel had established a new geographical unit—Earth. The world shrank, from an all-enveloping, immersive environment to a single unit of measure, a metric of distance, no more meaningful than an inch or a mile.

The postwar belief in the limitless possibilities of technology took its ultimate form in "astrofuturism," a kind of galactic Manifest Destiny. After World War II, Arthur C. Clarke proclaimed that "interplanetary travel is now the only form of 'conquest and empire' compatible with civilization." Space truly was the final frontier. In this view, reaching for the stars wasn't a way to embrace Earth; it was a means of quitting it altogether. "Let us forget the Earth," Ray Bradbury told an interviewer. "You can't stay in your mother's womb forever. . . . The only way the Earth can continue her life is by spitting you out, vomiting you up into the sky, beyond the atmosphere into worlds you cannot imagine." Will Mother Nature become an empty-nester?

Seeing the planet as a tiny thing reinforced paternal attitudes toward the environment that, in many, became an overinflated sense of self-importance. Norman Mailer summed up the Apollo program: "Now man had something with which to speak to God." From his perch in outer space, Frank Borman thought to himself, "This must be what God sees." Humanity had outgrown its cradle, transcending terra firma to become citizens of the stars, striding in the halls of the heavens.

From Planet to Landscape

The "more extreme forms of nationalism" that Clarke believed an image of Earth might vanquish are provincial struggles for political power and physical resources. Natural and human communities always transcend political divisions, and in the age of global warming, national boundaries have little bearing on the most pressing problems. In fact, ancient political borders are shifting as a *result* of global warming—Italy and Switzerland recently agreed to move their shared border 150 meters into Italian territory because melting alpine glaciers have altered the watershed that demarcates the two countries. As the planet heats up, it's reshaping nations.

"All ethics," wrote Aldo Leopold, "rest upon a single premise: that the individual is a member of a community of interdependent parts." Yet, while the "one Earth, one world" vision may be an inspired ethical idea, it's a disastrous aesthetic one. Economic globalization has metastasized into multinational corporations feeding on ancient peoples and places. The project Worldmapper portrays "the world as you've never seen it" by visualizing global and regional trends, and even a quick glance at maps representing population,

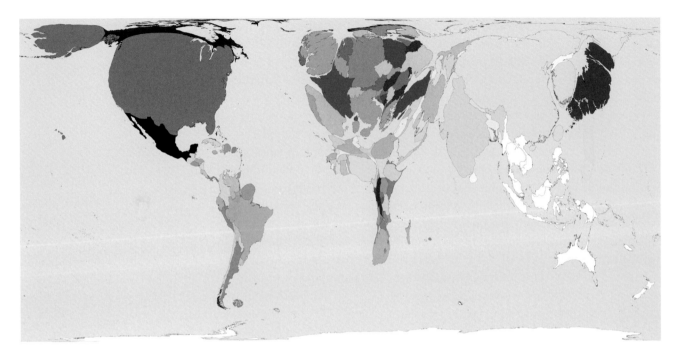

wealth, and the loss of resources and wildlife reveals a clear picture of the First World bleeding the Third World dry. Together, these images visualize a planet morphing into something lifeless, inert. Today, the biggest risk is not that Earth will give way to tribalism and special interests; it's that uniformity will extinguish difference.

> "The modern state is too large…to command the kind of affection that arises out of experience and intimate knowledge."
>
> —*Yi-Fu Tuan*

In Leopold's image of community, *interdependent* doesn't mean indistinguishable or identical, yet this is exactly the visual, spatial, and cultural outcome of globalization. Possibly the most significant perpetrator, the United States, long has promoted cultural assimilation as an ideal, and the social metaphor of the "melting pot" has become a physical reality that boils away the unique flavor of any place, producing a bland suburban soup the world over. Canada's

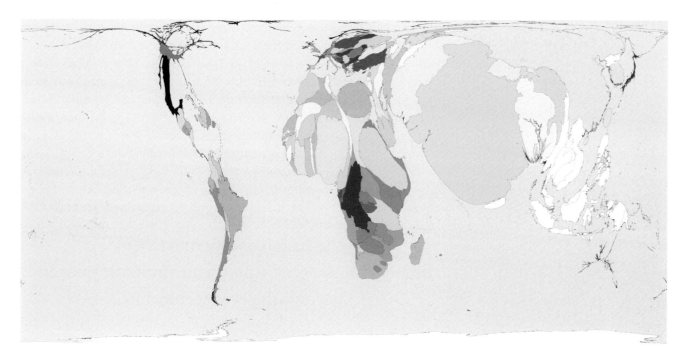

model of the cultural mosaic, which celebrates diversity within a variegated tapestry, might serve as a better vision for architecture and urbanism. The environmentalist's mantra, "Think Globally, Act Locally," can become the designer's mandate: *Global Ethics, Local Aesthetics*. One Earth, many worlds.

We might expand Leopold's sentiment to say that all aesthetics rest upon a single premise—that the individual place is the center of any community of interdependent parts. All things are connected, but all things begin on the present ground. According to author Robert Poole, images of Earth from the outside shifted the world's view "from landscape to planet," a fine ethical consequence half a century ago. Today, however, our aesthetic task is to return from planet to landscape, to rediscover the immersive, sensory experience of terrain. Clarke worried about nationalism's extreme allegiance to political entities and imagined communities. Now we need a different kind of patriotism, one born from allegiance to natural environments and experienced communities. Loyalty to the land can embrace the diversity of cultures, the individuality of place, and the singularity of setting.

Patriotism, writes the geographer Yi-Fu Tuan, means "the love of one's *terra patria* or natal land. In ancient times it was a strictly local sentiment." In modern times, particularly in the culture of "America first," few of us feel

The True Picture of the Planet. Worldmapper.org portrays "the world as you've never seen it" by visualizing global and regional trends. The size of a country's landmass is adjusted to reflect its statistical relationship to the topic. For example, the ecological footprint of the United States is bloated *(a)*, and its poverty is nearly nonexistent *(b)*.

any kind of kinship to a natal land, only to a national interest. Patriotism now suggests attachment to large-scale nation-states, an unnatural condition too abstract to embrace easily, as Tuan explains. "The modern state is too large, its boundaries too arbitrary, its area too heterogeneous to command the kind of affection that arises out of experience and intimate knowledge. Modern man has conquered distance but not time. In a life span, a man now—as in the past—can establish profound roots only in a small corner of the world." While the sight of the entire Earth brought about a new perspective and helped expand humanity's attention beyond national boundaries, today places would benefit from telescoping inward and collapsing our point of view to what the eye actually witnesses and the body directly senses.

The sustainability movement began with imagery—powerful, dramatic imagery like nothing ever seen before.

New Visions

The sustainability movement began with imagery—powerful, dramatic imagery like nothing ever seen before. Yet, in our pursuit of sustainability, the power of imagery has faded from memory. In our focus on the inner workings of things over their outer appearances, iconography has given way to technology. But the Apollo photographs demonstrate how profoundly image can inspire ethics. Likewise, aesthetics can promote action. Imagery inspired the environmental movement, which in turn can create great imagery. Design can influence and implement both how we see the world and how we interact with it, for the shape of things reflects and reinforces both our views and our values.

Aesthetic understanding has everything to do with environmental intelligence. The links—or lack thereof—between culture and nature, between people and place, have a profound impact on our lives. We can ignore those relationships, or we can build on them to generate more meaning and relevance. Everything we create can help preserve resources (Conservation), bring pleasure (Attraction), and promote shared identity (Connection). With new knowledge emerging all the time, it has become both easier and more urgent for designers to draw on collective intelligence over individual taste. Wisdom spanning many generations, combined with new research and techniques, makes a potent arsenal.

At the beginning of this book, I asked whether we can become as smart about the way things *look* as we are becoming about the way they *work*—whether designers can embrace aesthetics based on intelligence, not intuition. I hope by now it's clear not just that we can but that we must. To answer the questions of sustainability, design must become less about personal preference and more about public—and planetary—benefit.

Could every image designers create change our thinking, as the first photographs of the whole Earth did? Can a city reimagine the shape of the world, as Fuller's atlas and Worldmapper do? Can a car, chair, cup, or spoon inspire new habits, and can a building encourage us to embrace the places around us—just by offering up smarter, richer images? They can, and they should. I can think of no greater vision for design than this—to learn from the entire intelligence of Earth how to put down roots in each "small corner of the world."

What a beautiful world we could make.

Parabola Architecture.
Timepiece House, Charlottesville, Virginia.

Epilogue: A Beauty Manifesto

[Design means] changing existing situations into preferred ones.

—Herbert Simon

Ten principles for advancing an aesthetics of ecology. Every designer everywhere can:

1. Bridge the divide between "good design" and "green design"

2. Turn beauty and sustainability into the same thing

3. Erase the distinction between how things look and how things work

4. Break down the walls between the arts and sciences

5. Adopt the three principles:

   Conserve: **Shape things to respect resources**

   Attract: **Shape things to be easy to use and deeply satisfying**

   Connect: **Shape things to embrace place**

6. Start with the napkin sketch, not the technical manual

7. Develop a scientific method for design

8. Strengthen the ties between form and performance, between image and endurance

9. Make things to work as well and to last as long as they should

10. Make things better

Acknowledgments

T<small>HIS BOOK WAS A LONG TIME COMING</small>.

Many years ago, when I first heard the phrase "sustainable design," my first question was, "What does it look like?" At first, I got the impression that this was an irrelevant, even naive way of thinking, but over time I came to believe that it's as important a question as any. Because few have offered any answer at all, much less a satisfying one, I set out to address it myself. What I offer here is not nearly comprehensive, but I hope it provokes more dialogue—and more questions.

Along the way, I've had too many conversations with too many people to acknowledge all of them properly, but my thanks go out to all of you.

The American Institute of Architects' RFP program funded early research, as did the Michael Kalil Endowment for Smart Design, at Parsons The New School for Design. Jean Gardner, at Parsons, is a treasure.

I completed the manuscript during a residency on Lake Como, at the Rockefeller Foundation's Bellagio Center, the best-kept secret in the world of arts and letters. Thanks to John Cary for recommending it, and thanks to Pilar Palacia and the other residents—Carole, Duane, Yotam, Claire, Rita, Barbara, David, Christina, Kate, George, and others—who made my time there unforgettable. Pondering beauty is easy in a place of such exquisite beauty.

Ned Cramer, Amanda Kolson Hurley, and Braulio Agnese, of *Architect* magazine, encouraged me to toy with these ideas in my monthly column from 2007 to 2010.

From 2008 to 2010, Susan Inglis and Margaret Casey, of the Sustainable Furnishings Council and the World Market Center, enthusiastically supported and sponsored the "One Good Chair" competition, our attempt to encourage this book's ideas among young furniture designers. Thanks go to the competition's many judges and designers for their time and attention.

Heather Boyer at Island Press worked hard to get this published and patiently listened to my crazy ideas about how the book's design might demonstrate its principles. Art director Maureen Gately and cover designer Milan Bozic both were essential in giving shape to this book about shape.

Many, many audiences encouraged and challenged me in lectures and discussions around the world. And many friends and colleagues gave me special insight or inspiration: Michelle Amt, Pete O'Shea, Susan Szenasy, Mark Rylander, Marc L'Italien, Henry Siegel, Nadav Malin, Lou Boza, Matthew Geiss, Kate Bakewell, Dana Bourland, Jackie Decter, Traci Rose Rider, Don Watson, Jason McLennan, Carrie and Kevin Burke, Craig Schwitter, Byron Stigge, Matthew Herman, Adam Yarinsky, Guy Nordenson, Steve Kieran, James Timberlake, Michelle Addington, Bill McDonough, Richard Taylor, Jim Wise, Judi Heerwagen, Dayna Baumeister, Janine Benyus, Gail Vittori, Pliny Fisk, Guy Gleysteen, and the staff and board of directors of GreenBlue.

Big love, as always, to Kira Gould, for your perfect ear, your unflagging support, and your enduring friendship. You're the best.

Finally, there's Harold Roth. Long ago, he tried to convince me that it's all about beauty. He was right.

I dedicate this book to my family, who brought me back to life; and to Kate, who brought me back to love. You are my heart.

Selected References

Abram, David. *The Spell of the Sensuous: Perception and Language in a More-than-Human World.* New York: Random House, 1997.

Ackerman, Diane. *A Natural History of the Senses.* New York: Vintage, 1990.

Alexander, Christopher. "A City Is Not A Tree." *Architectural Forum* 122, no. 1 (April 1965): 58–62.

———. *A Pattern Language: Towns, Buildings, Construction.* New York: Oxford University Press, 1977.

———. *The Nature of Order: An Essay on the Art of Building and the Nature of the Universe.* Berkeley, CA: CES Publishing, 2001.

Appleton, Jay. *The Experience of Landscape.* New York: Wiley, 1975.

Banham, Reyner. *The Architecture of the Well-Tempered Environment.* Chicago: University of Chicago Press, 1984.

Barabási, Albert-László. *Linked: The New Science of Networks.* New York: Perseus Books Group, 2002.

Basalla, George. *The Evolution of Technology.* New York: Cambridge University Press, 1989.

Batty, Michael, and Paul Longley. *Fractal Cities.* London: Academic Press, 1994.

Bejan, Adrian. "The Golden Ratio Predicted: Vision, Cognition and Locomotion as a Single Design in Nature." *International Journal of Design & Nature and Ecodynamics* 4, no. 2 (2009): 97–104.

Birren, Faber. *Color and Human Response: Aspects of Light and Color Bearing on the Reactions of Living Things and the Welfare of Human Beings.* New York: Wiley, 1984.

Brundtland, Gro Harlem, et al. *Our Common Future.* New York: World Commission on Environment and Development, 1987.

Busch, Akiko. *The Uncommon Life of Common Objects.* New York: Metropolis Books, 2005.

Canizaro, Vincent. *Architectural Regionalism: Collected Writings on Place, Identity, Modernity, and Tradition.* New York: Princeton Architectural Press, 2007.

Carson, Rachel. *The Sense of Wonder.* New York: HarperCollins, 1956.

Cranz, Galen. *The Chair: Rethinking Culture, Body, and Design.* New York: Norton, 2000.

Dubos, René. *The Wooing of Earth.* London: Athlone Press, 1980.

Dutton, Denis. *The Art Instinct: Beauty, Pleasure, and Human Evolution.* New York: Bloomsbury Press, 2009.

Fletcher, Kate. "Clothes That Connect." In *Designers, Visionaries and Other Stories: A Collection of Sustainable Design Essays,* ed. Jonathan Chapman and Nick Gant. London: Routledge, 2007.

Florida, Richard. *Who's Your City? How the Creative Economy Is Making Where to Live the Most Important Decision of Your Life.* New York: Basic Books, 2008.

Fuller, R. Buckminster. *Nine Chains to the Moon.* Carbondale: Southern Illinois University Press, 1966.

Gladwell, Malcolm. *Blink: The Power of Thinking without Thinking.* New York: Back Bay Books, 2007.

Heerwagen, Judith, and James Wise. "The Ecologic of Color, Pattern, and Texture." Internal report prepared for Herman Miller (1997).

Heschong, Lisa. *Thermal Delight in Architecture.* Cambridge, MA: MIT Press, 1979.

Hildebrand, Grant. *The Origins of Architectural Pleasure.* Berkeley, CA: University of California Press, 1999.

Hitchcock, Henry-Russell, and Philip Johnson. *The International Style.* New York: Norton, 1997.

Hosey, Lance. "Hearing Voices." *Metropolis,* May 2002, 60, 62.

———. "Green Design: All Skin and No Bones?" *Architecture,* August 2005, 21–22, 24.

———. Monthly "ECO" column. *Architect,* April 2007–December 2010.

Jacobs, Jane. *The Death and Life of Great American Cities.* New York: Random House, 1961.

Kellert, Stephen R., Judith Heerwagen, and Martin Mador. *Biophilic Design: The Theory, Science and Practice of Bringing Buildings to Life.* Hoboken, NJ: Wiley, 2008.

Khaslavsky, Julie, and Nathan Shedroff. "Understanding the Seductive Experience." *Communications of the ACM* (1999).

Kunstler, James Howard. *The Geography of Nowhere: The Rise and Decline of America's Man-Made Landscape.* New York: Free Press, 1994.

Lanham, Richard A. *The Economics of Attention: Style and Substance in the Age of Information.* Chicago: University of Chicago Press, 2006.

Leopold, Aldo. *A Sand County Almanac: And Sketches Here and There.* New York: Oxford University Press, 1949.

Lidwell, William, Kritina Holden, and Jill Butler. *Universal Principles of Design.* Minneapolis: Rockport, 2003.

Logan, William Bryant. *Dirt: The Ecstatic Skin of the Earth.* New York: Norton, 2007.

Louv, Richard. *The Last Child in the Woods: Saving Our Children from Nature-Deficit Disorder.* New York: Algonquin Books, 2008.

Lynch, Kevin. *The Image of the City.* Cambridge, MA: MIT Press, 1960.

Mandelbrot, Benoit. *The Fractal Geometry of Nature.* New York: Freeman, 1982.

Meadows, Donella H., Dennis L. Meadows, Jorgen Randers, and William W. Behrens III. *The Limits to Growth.* New York: Universe Books, 1972.

Naisbitt, John. *High Tech/High Touch: Technology and Our Search for Meaning.* London: Nicholas Brealey, 2001.

Neuwirth, Robert. *Shadow Cities: A Billion Squatters, A New Urban World.* New York: Routledge, 2004.

Norberg-Schulz, Christian. *Nightlands: Nordic Building.* Cambridge, MA: MIT Press, 1997.

Norman, Donald. *Emotional Design: Why We Love (or Hate) Everyday Things.* New York: Basic Books, 2005.

Orr, David. *Ecological Literacy: Education and the Transition to a Postmodern World.* Albany, NY: SUNY Press, 1992.

Pallasmaa, Juhani. *The Eyes of the Skin: Architecture and the Senses.* London: Academy Press, 2005.

Parker, Andrew. *In the Blink of an Eye: How Vision Sparked the Big Bang of Evolution.* New York: Basic Books, 2004.

Pollan, Michael. *The Botany of Desire.* New York: Random House, 2002.

Poole, Robert. *Earthrise: How Man First Saw the Earth.* New Haven, CT: Yale University Press, 2010.

Postrel, Virginia. *The Substance of Style: How the Rise of Aesthetic Value Is Remaking Commerce, Culture, and Consciousness.* New York: HarperCollins, 2004.

Ramachandran, Vilayanur S., and Diane Rogers-Ramachandran. "The Neurology of Aesthetics." *Scientific American Mind,* October/November 2006.

Salingaros, Nikos. *A Theory of Architecture.* Wilmington, DE: ISI Distributed Titles, 2007.

————. *Principles of Urban Structure.* Amsterdam: Techne Press, 2005.

Schlosser, Eric. *Fast Food Nation: The Dark Side of the All-American Meal.* New York: HarperCollins, 2004.

Schumacher, E. F. *Small Is Beautiful: Economics as if People Mattered.* 25th anniversary ed. Vancouver, BC: Hartley & Marks, 1999.

Schwartz, Barry. *The Paradox of Choice: Why More Is Less.* New York: Harper Perennial, 2005.

Shiva, Vandana. *Earth Democracy: Justice, Sustainability and Peace*. London: Zed Books, 2006.

Slade, Giles, *Made to Break: Technology and Obsolescence in America*. Cambridge, MA: Harvard University Press, 2007.

Sperling, Bert, and Peter J. Sander. *Cities Ranked & Rated*. Hoboken, NJ: Wiley, 2004.

Suzuki, David. *The Sacred Balance: Rediscovering Our Place in Nature*. Vancouver, BC: Greystone Books, 2007.

Tanizaki, Jun'ichirō. *In Praise of Shadows*. New Haven, CT: Leete's Island Books, 1977.

Taylor, Richard, et al. "Fractal Expressionism." *Physics World* 12, no. 10 (1999): 25.

———. "Universal Aesthetic of Fractals." *Chaos and Graphics* 27 (2003): 813.

Tuan, Yi-Fu. *Topophilia: A Study of Environmental Perception, Attitudes, and Values*. New York: Columbia University Press, 1990.

Wilson, Edward O. *Biophilia*. Cambridge, MA: Harvard University Press, 1984.

———. *Consilience: The Unity of Knowledge*. New York: Vintage, 1999.

Illustration and Photograph Credits

Chapter 1

Page xii: JDGrant / Dreamstime.com

Page 4 (top): Renzo Piano Building Workshop

Page 4 (bottom): Ishida Shunji, Renzo Piano Building Workshop

Chapter 2

Page 12 (top): Lee Snider / Dreamstime.com

Page 12 (middle): MlHead / Dreamstime.com

Page 12 (bottom): Ignacio Ciocchini

Page 15: Thayyilani / Dreamstime.com

Page 16: Allison Achauer / Dreamstime.com; Lance Hosey

Page 17 (top): Tata Motors

Page 17 (bottom): Alchemy LLC

Page 18: Joris Laarman Lab

Page 19: Natalia Matveeva / Dreamstime.com

Chapter 3

Page 30 (top): Ecofont.com

Page 30 (middle): Meeker & Associates

Page 30 (bottom): Berlin Partner GmbH - *be* Berlin

Page 36 (left): 2011 Daimler AG. All rights reserved

Page 36 (right): MIT / Franco Vairani

Page 38: Gensler

Page 43 (top): Viorel Sima / Dreamstime.com

Page 43 (bottom): Gors4730 / Dreamstime.com

Page 46 (top): Frank Ockert

Page 46 (middle): Darren Petrucci

Page 46 (bottom): Cook+Fox Architects

Page 48 (top): Fabio Cardano / Dreamstime.com

Page 48 (middle): Sova004 / Dreamstime.com

Page 48 (bottom): National Oceanic and Atmospheric Administration

Page 51: William Vassal

Page 53: Robert Corser

Chapter 4

Page 54: Institute for Forestry and Nature Research Wageningen, The Netherlands; Architect: Stefan Behnisch,; Photographer: Stefan Behnisch, Frank Ockert

Page 57 (right): Pixac / Dreamstime.com

Page 62: AMID.cero9

Page 66: Michael Roopenian

Page 67: KONYK

Page 72: fuseproject

Chapter 5

Page 74: Ateliers Jean Nouvel

Page 76: Denancé Michel

Page 78: Prakash Patel

Page 83: Adapted from Lidwell, et al, *Universal Principles of Design*

Page 86: Javarman / Dreamstime.com

Page 89: Richard Taylor

Page 91: Thom Faulders

Page 92: SOM

Chapter 6

Page 94 (top four): Jittasak Narknisorn

Page 94 (bottom two): Eric Tong

Page 97 (left): Murat Cokeker / Dreamstime.com

Page 97 (right): Kokandr / Dreamstime.com

Page 103 (left): Nokia

Page 103 (right): AREAWARE

Page 105: fuseproject

Page 106 (left): Aoyoshi Company, Ltd, Japan

Page 106 (right): Fredrik Ottosson

Chapter 7

Page 116 (left): Lance Hosey

Page 116 (right): Thomas Lewandovski

Page 122: Lance Hosey, using these image sources: Tomasz Bidermann / Dreamstime.com; Anthony Berenyi / Dreamstime.com; Gerry Boughan / Dreamstime.com; Erin Janssen / Dreamstime.com; Carol McKinney Highsmith, Wikimedia

Page 128 (top): Paul Hester

Page 128 (bottom): Nic Lehoux

Page 131 (top): HalkinPhotograph LLC/Barry Halkin

Page 131 (bottom): Kieran Timberlake

Page 132: Anthony Browell, courtesy of the Architecture Foundation Australia

Page 135: Sean Dorsy

Page 136 & 137: Mark West, University of Manitoba

Page 139: Nigel Young / Foster + Partners

Chapter 8

Page 142: Foster + Partners

Page 148: Dave Cooksey

Page 153: Michael Sorkin Studio

Page 156: Images and concept by de Urbanisten

Page 159: Guy Nordenson and Associates; Catherine Seavitt Studio; Architecture Research Office

Page 160: Fougeron Architecture

Page 163: Megumi / Dreamstime.com

Chapter 9

Page 166: Courtesy of NASA

Page 170: Eric Gaba

Page 174: SASI Group, University of Sheffield; Mark Newman, University of Michigan

Index

Page numbers followed by "f" indicate figures.